"David Dockery and Timothy Geo[...]ed service in both church and academ[...]m-mendation of the Christian intellec[...][...]pe-rienced, trustworthy, and encouraging. It is a book to enjoy both in itself and as a welcome guide to much, much more."

> **Mark A. Noll,** Francis A. McAnaney Professor of History,
> University of Notre Dame

"David Dockery and Timothy George are among the preeminent Christian intellectuals of the current age. This book demonstrates why. The volume courses with biblical conviction, evangelical vitality, and a breadth that inter-acts with the great cloud of witnesses from every place and era of the church of Jesus Christ. I commend this book heartily to students, professors, and church leaders."

> **Russell D. Moore,** President, Ethics and Religious Liberty
> Commission of the Southern Baptist Convention

"In a clear and concise presentation of the great thinkers of the church, the authors of this book launch a new series that promises to provide students with an impor-tant key to unlock the treasure store of the Christian tradition. They show us once again how exciting Christianity is and why it has captured the minds of succes-sive generations. At a time when our faith is being challenged as never before, this introduction to its riches promises to equip the saints of the next generation to claim their inheritance and extend it further to the glory of God."

> **Gerald Bray,** Distinguished Professor of Historical Theology,
> Knox Theological Seminary

"This appeal to Christian educators to take the great tradition of Christian thinking much more seriously, to find our place within it, and to renew it today has arrived in the nick of time. For despite the common invocation of 'integration' language at our Christian universities, our schools are all too often led by pragmatists beholden to the forces of the market more than the life of the Christian mind. David Dockery and Timothy George herein remind us of our heritage, our very reason for being. I pray that God will use their efforts in the lives of countless students, teachers, and Christian college leaders, inspiring passionate commitment to the values and the virtues that attracted us to Christian education in the first place."

> **Douglas A. Sweeney,** Professor of Church History,
> Trinity Evangelical Divinity School

"David Dockery and Timothy George have written a compelling volume that makes a strong case for the pivotal role that the Christian intellectual tradition should fulfill in a serious liberal arts education. Although the volume was written as a student's text, individuals who care about Christian higher education (administrators, faculty, and trustees) will benefit from reading and applying the principles articulated in this thoughtful work."

Kim S. Phipps, President, Messiah College

"Don't be misled by the modesty of this book's title. While the book surely is a winsome and accessible introduction to the subject for any inquiring student, it has much more than that to offer. Its authors are two of the most eminent figures in the field of Christian higher education, and their book reflects the immense range of their learning and experience, even though it wears its learning lightly. The result is a compact but powerful work that will be an invaluable tool for all of us who wrestle with the great task of integrating faith and learning and of showing others how the good, the true, and the beautiful find their ultimate source and meaning in God."

Wilfred M. McClay, SunTrust Chair of Excellence in Humanities, University of Tennessee at Chattanooga

"David Dockery and Timothy George, two experienced and wise Christian educators, have produced the first volume of what promises to be an important series of guides—aimed at students—intended both to recover and instruct regarding the Christian intellectual tradition. This volume, and no doubt the series as well, meets a significant need, not only for students but also for ministers and academics who are charged with the responsibility of helping us all think and live faithfully as followers of Christ. In light of our deeply flawed world, every generation needs a fresh retelling—in literature, theology, the arts, philosophy, or public policy—of the central truths of all human and natural experience, as revealed by the one true and living God through his Son and as authoritatively and indispensably taught in Holy Scripture."

Robert B. Sloan, President, Houston Baptist University

ENDORSEMENTS FOR THE SERIES

"*Reclaiming the Christian Intellectual Tradition* is an exciting project that will freshly introduce readers to the riches of historic Christian thought and practice. As the modern secular academy struggles to reclaim a semblance of purpose, this series demonstrates why a deeply rooted Christian worldview offers an intellectual coherence so badly needed in our fragmented culture. Assembling a formidable cohort of respected evangelical scholars, this volume promises to supply must-read orientations to the disciplines for the next generation of Christian students."

Thomas Kidd, Department of History, Baylor University

"To say that this project is overdue is perhaps the understatement of the century. I'm grateful that David Dockery and Timothy George, two exemplars of the Christian intellectual tradition, are blazing this trail for us. Many of us have been the happy beneficiaries of their scholarship over the past two decades; many will be the appreciative heirs of their work as this series develops."

Andrew Westmoreland, President, Samford University

"This new series is exactly what Christian higher education needs to shore up its intellectual foundations for the challenges of the coming decades. Whether students are studying in professedly Christian institutions or in more traditionally secular settings, these volumes will provide a firm basis from which to withstand the dismissive attitude toward biblical thinking that seems so pervasive in the academy today. These titles will make their way onto the required reading lists at Christian colleges and universities as they seek to ensure a firm biblical perspective for students, regardless of discipline. Similarly, pastors on secular campuses will find this series to be an invaluable bibliography for guiding students who are struggling with coalescing their emerging intellectual curiosity with their developing faith."

Carl E. Zylstra, Executive Director, Association of Reformed Colleges and Universities

✚ RECLAIMING THE CHRISTIAN INTELLECTUAL TRADITION

David S. Dockery, series editor

CONSULTING EDITORS

Hunter Baker
Timothy George
Neil Nielson
Philip G. Ryken
Michael J. Wilkins
John D. Woodbridge

OTHER RCIT VOLUMES

Art and Music, Paul Munson and Joshua Farris Drake

Biblical and Theological Studies, Michael J. Wilkins and Erik Thoennes

Christian Worldview, Philip G. Ryken

Economics, Greg Forster

Education, Ted Newell

Ethics and Moral Reasoning, C. Ben Mitchell

The Great Tradition of Christian Thinking, David S. Dockery and Timothy George

History, Nathan A. Finn

The Liberal Arts, Gene C. Fant Jr.

Literature, Louis Markos

Media, Journalism, and Communication, Read Mercer Schuchardt

The Natural Sciences, John A. Bloom

Philosophy, David K. Naugle

Political Thought, Hunter Baker

Psychology, Stanton L. Jones

RECLAIMING THE
CHRISTIAN INTELLECTUAL TRADITION

THE GREAT TRADITION OF CHRISTIAN THINKING
A STUDENT'S GUIDE

David S. Dockery &
Timothy George

Series Editor: David S. Dockery

WHEATON, ILLINOIS

The Great Tradition of Christian Thinking: A Student's Guide

Copyright © 2012 by David S. Dockery and Timothy George

Published by Crossway
        1300 Crescent Street
        Wheaton, Illinois 60187

Cover design: Jon McGrath, Simplicated Studio

First printing 2012

Printed in the United States of America

Unless otherwise indicated, scripture quotations are from the ESV® Bible (The Holy Bible, English Standard Version®), copyright © 2001 by Crossway, a publishing ministry of Good News Publishers. Used by permission. All rights reserved.

Scripture quotations marked AT are the authors' translation.

Trade paperback ISBN: 978-1-4335-2513-1
PDF ISBN: 978-1-4335-2515-5
Mobipocket ISBN: 978-1-4335-2864-4
ePub ISBN: 978-1-4335-3488-1

Library of Congress Cataloging-in-Publication Data

The great tradition of Christian thinking : a student's guide / David S. Dockery and Timothy George, editors.
    p. cm.
  Includes bibliographical references and index.
  ISBN 978-1-4335-2513-1 (tp)
  1. Church history. 2. Christianity. 3. College students--Religious life. 4. Education, Humanistic--Curricula. I. Dockery, David S. II. George, Timothy.
BR145.3.G74   2012
230.09—dc23   2011045934

Crossway is a publishing ministry of Good News Publishers.

5L		31	30	29	28	27	26	25	24	23	22	21
15	14	13	12	11	10	9	8	7	6	5	4	3

To

Bob Agee, president,
Oklahoma Baptist University, 1982–1998

Clyde Cook, *in memoriam*, president,
Biola University, 1982–2007

Jay Kesler, president,
Taylor University, 1985–2000

Duane Litfin, president,
Wheaton College, 1993–2010

Remarkable leaders,
Special friends,
Treasured colleagues and mentors

CONTENTS

SERIES PREFACE

The Reclaiming the Christian Intellectual Tradition series is designed to provide an overview of the distinctive way the church has read the Bible, formulated doctrine, provided education, and engaged the culture. The contributors to this series all agree that personal faith and genuine Christian piety are essential for the life of Christ followers and for the church. These contributors also believe that helping others recognize the importance of serious thinking about God, Scripture, and the world needs a renewed emphasis at this time in order that the truth claims of the Christian faith can be passed along from one generation to the next. The study guides in this series will enable us to see afresh how the Christian faith shapes how we live, how we think, how we write books, how we govern society, and how we relate to one another in our churches and social structures. The richness of the Christian intellectual tradition provides guidance for the complex challenges that believers face in this world.

This series is particularly designed for Christian students and others associated with college and university campuses, including faculty, staff, trustees, and other various constituents. The contributors to the series will explore how the Bible has been interpreted in the history of the church, as well as how theology has been formulated. They will ask: How does the Christian faith influence our understanding of culture, literature, philosophy, government, beauty, art, or work? How does the Christian intellectual tradition help us understand truth? How does the Christian intellectual tradition shape our approach to education? We believe that this series is not only timely but that it meets an important need, because the secular culture in which we now find ourselves is, at best, indifferent to the Christian faith, and the Christian world—at least in its more popular forms—tends to be confused about the beliefs, heritage, and tradition associated with the Christian faith.

At the heart of this work is the challenge to prepare a generation of Christians to think Christianly, to engage the academy and the culture, and to serve church and society. We believe that both the breadth and the depth of the Christian intellectual tradition need to be reclaimed, revitalized, renewed, and revived for us to carry forward this work. These study guides will seek to provide a framework to help introduce students to the great tradition of Christian thinking, seeking to highlight its importance for understanding the world, its significance for serving both church and society, and its application for Christian thinking and learning. The series is a starting point for exploring important ideas and issues such as truth, meaning, beauty, and justice.

We trust that the series will help introduce readers to the apostles, church fathers, Reformers, philosophers, theologians, historians, and a wide variety of other significant thinkers. In addition to well-known leaders such as Clement, Origen, Augustine, Thomas Aquinas, Martin Luther, and Jonathan Edwards, readers will be pointed to William Wilberforce, G. K. Chesterton, T. S. Eliot, Dorothy Sayers, C. S. Lewis, Johann Sebastian Bach, Isaac Newton, Johannes Kepler, George Washington Carver, Elizabeth Fox-Genovese, Michael Polanyi, Henry Luke Orombi, and many others. In doing so, we hope to introduce those who throughout history have demonstrated that it is indeed possible to be serious about the life of the mind while simultaneously being deeply committed Christians. These efforts to strengthen serious Christian thinking and scholarship will not be limited to the study of theology, scriptural interpretation, or philosophy, even though these areas provide the framework for understanding the Christian faith for all other areas of exploration. In order for us to reclaim and advance the Christian intellectual tradition, we must have some understanding of the tradition itself. The volumes in this series will seek to explore this tradition and its application for our twenty-first-century world. Each volume contains a glossary, study questions, and a list of resources for further study, which we trust will provide helpful guidance for our readers.

I am deeply grateful to the series editorial committee: Timothy George, John Woodbridge, Michael Wilkins, Niel Nielson, Philip Ryken, and Hunter Baker. Each of these colleagues joins me in thanking our various contributors for their fine work. We all express our appreciation to Justin Taylor, Jill Carter, Allan Fisher, Lane Dennis, and the Crossway team for their enthusiastic support for the project. We offer the project with the hope that students will be helped, faculty and Christian leaders will be encouraged, institutions will be strengthened, and churches will be built up, and, ultimately, that God will be glorified.

Soli Deo Gloria
David S. Dockery,
Series Editor

AUTHORS' PREFACE

The opportunity to work together on another significant project is a privilege that we do not take for granted. Over the past twenty years we have participated together in nearly a dozen publications; the one you hold in your hands will be the fourth book that we have coauthored or coedited. In many ways our work on this project began even before that first coedited work in 1990.

In God's good providence we had the privilege of being introduced to one another in 1987 when David was invited to serve as a visiting faculty member for the summer term at The Southern Baptist Theological Seminary in Louisville, Kentucky, where Timothy already held a full-time appointment in the area of historical theology. That summer was the first of dozens and dozens of conversations that have followed since that time, many over lunch at one of Timothy's favorite Mexican restaurants, about the nature and ideals of Christian higher education, as well as theological education. In 1988 Timothy was named the founding dean of the Beeson Divinity School on the campus of Samford University. Shortly thereafter, David was named dean and vice president at The Southern Baptist Seminary in Louisville, where he served until moving to Union University about sixteen years ago to serve as president. As can be seen, our lives for the past twenty-five years have been closely connected and bound up with institutions associated with the work of what is often called the Christian intellectual tradition.

The series for which this volume serves as the introductory work is called Reclaiming the Christian Intellectual Tradition. Some of our initial publications, which were shaped by those earlier conversations, have been influential in what we have presented in this little book, which we have titled *The Great Tradition of*

Christian Thinking. That thinking was exemplarily modeled by the major Reformers in the sixteenth century and described in Timothy's publication called *Theology of the Reformers* (1988). David published a work called *Biblical Interpretation Then and Now* (1992), which looked at key turning points in biblical interpretation throughout the history of the church. The great thinkers represented in those two volumes have again surfaced as the primary shapers to which we have given much attention in this initial volume in this new Crossway series. It is our hope that the new presentation of these leaders who have shaped so many aspects of church history and Christian theology will encourage many to join us in the effort to seek to reclaim and advance the Christian intellectual tradition. It is our prayer not just to recover and present key aspects of Christian thought and history but to do so with the goal of strengthening the work of the people of God in the churches and particularly in Christian academic communities.

This work would not have taken place without the wonderful support of many people. We want to thank the Crossway team for their encouragement and enablement in this project; particularly we wish to express appreciation to Justin Taylor, Lydia Brownback, Jill Carter, Allan Fisher, and Lane Dennis. We also want to express our deep gratitude to Le-Ann Little, B. Coyne, and Cindy Meredith for their assistance. Our genuine thanksgiving is offered to Melanie Rickman, who has invested untold hours in this project. Without her tireless efforts, this work would have never seen the light of day. We also wish to thank our colleagues at Union University and Beeson Divinity School for their help and support along the way, as well as the editorial team for their oversight for this series.

Timothy also wishes to thank Denise, and David offers his gratitude to Lanese. We are blessed by their love, prayers, and support through yet another publishing project.

We have dedicated this volume to four men who have served as role models, friends, mentors, and guides for our work in the field of higher education. We offer thanksgiving to God for the ministry and influence of Bob Agee, Clyde Cook, Jay Kesler, and Duane Litfin. Ultimately, we offer this volume with the prayer that readers will be helped, that Christian institutions will be strengthened, that the gospel will be advanced, and that our great and majestic God will be glorified.

Soli Deo Gloria
David S. Dockery
Timothy George

1

THE BEGINNING OF THE GREAT TRADITION

THE INTERPRETATION OF SCRIPTURE

There can be no Christian intellectual life without reference to
the writings of the prophets and evangelists, the doctrines of the
church fathers, the conceptual niceties of the scholastics, the language of the liturgy, the songs of the poets and hymn writers,
the exploits of the martyrs, and the holy tales of the saints.

Robert L. Wilken, "The Christian Intellectual Tradition," *First Things* (1991)

All that is meant by tradition, then, is the faithful handing down
from generation to generation of scripture interpretation consensu-
ally received worldwide and cross-culturally through two millennia.

Thomas C. Oden, *The Rebirth of Orthodoxy* (2003)

The calendars at the universities where we serve are filled with special events and activities, including dinners, banquets, receptions,
and open-house gatherings. One of the privileges that is ours at the
beginning of each semester is to invite new students to our homes,
where we have opportunity to meet these young men and women
and introduce them to other campus leaders. From these introduc-
tions, new relationships are started, and mentoring opportunities
begin. At other times during the year, we open our homes for a sea-
sonal open house, a gathering of faculty, staff, friends, donors, and
trustees. On this occasion it is a treat to welcome them and introduce trustees to faculty, and staff to friends from the community.

A joyful moment occurs for us when an interesting conversation develops and a new friendship is formed. Those examples seem to me to symbolize and demonstrate what is involved in the experience of reclaiming the Christian intellectual tradition.

This book and the books to follow in this series, in some way, serve as hosts and hostesses to a two-thousand-year-old open house. We want to invite readers to join us in this conversation as we introduce Augustine and Clement and Alexandria, Erasmus and Luther, Lewis, Bach, Kepler, and Chesterton. We are hopeful that readers will join us in this enormously rich and immense conversation with people from different places and periods of times.

The Great Tradition of Christian Thinking will introduce readers to the distinctive way that Christians through the years have read the Bible, formulated doctrine, provided education, and engaged the culture. At the heart of this volume and others in the series is the challenge to prepare a generation of Christians to think Christianly, to engage the academy and the culture, and to serve church and society. We believe that both the breadth and the depth of the Christian intellectual tradition need to be reclaimed, revitalized, renewed, and revived to carry forward this work. We will seek to provide a framework to help introduce students to the great tradition of Christian thinking, seeking to highlight its importance for understanding the world, its significance for serving both church and society, and its application for Christian thinking and learning, which reflects the heart of Christian higher education. We believe that insights gained from the Christian intellectual tradition will provide guidance for many of the complex challenges that Christ followers face in this world.

In his 1986 autobiographical work, *Confessions of a Theologian*, Carl F. H. Henry, dean of twentieth-century American evangelical theologians, lamented that several Christian colleges and universities had started to veer away from the centrality of their work, by and large giving up the cognitive focus on Christian thought in favor of Christian piety and activism. While we applaud all faithful efforts of Christian piety and activism, we believe Christian higher education has a distinctive role to play as the academic arm of the kingdom of God. We need not be forced to choose between head, heart, and hands while recognizing the important role of Christian higher education in engaging the great thinkers and ideas of history in order to frame our thoughts and responses to the issues of our day. It may well be that there is some connection with Henry's observation and that of the respondents to the 2011 survey of the Pew Forum on Religion and Public Life. More than nine out of ten of the 2,200 Christian leaders in the survey prioritized secular thinking as the major threat to the Christian movement around the world in the twenty-first century.

In 1994 Douglas Sloan published a most insightful volume called *Faith and Knowledge* in which he explored the path by which faith and knowledge have come to be treated as two entirely separate spheres of activity in the modern university. He traces the developments in academic circles over the past two hundred years that have led most men and women to envision faith as essentially a private matter, leaving Christianity's truth claims inaccessible to, or impenetrable by, rational knowledge. For two thousand years, the large majority of Christians have considered the truths of the Christian faith to be foundational for human flourishing and for a right relationship with God. Most universities in Europe and North America, however, now see the work of discovering and communicating knowledge as something completely separated from any connection to the Christian faith, even though many of these academic institutions can trace their beginning days to a Christian heritage. Those who follow in these Enlightenment and post-Enlightenment trajectories have started to raise additional questions regarding these issues.

The result, according to Sloan's vivid account, reflects the sad perspective held by many modern people, including many

Christians, that human knowledge and faith are basically disconnected, functioning in two separate spheres. Thus, academic contexts of influence tend to exist without reference to matters of faith. Similarly, and most unfortunately, many Christians and Christian institutions live with a concept of faith that is separate from and devoid of any sense of cognitive content.

While the accounts from the Pew Forum, Douglas Sloan, and Carl Henry have no obvious recognizable connections and no chronological affinities, they all, nevertheless, are obviously related by the problem of the faith/knowledge or faith/reason dichotomy. If faith is understood only in pious or activist terms, separating head from heart and hands, then we lack the framework to engage the challenging ideas and issues of our time within a Christian vantage point.

What is needed is a way to explore these matters by "thinking in Christian categories," to borrow a phrase from T. S. Eliot. Douglas Sloan's work clearly reveals the widely held perspective that knowledge is a cognitive matter, while faith is not. The result is what George Marsden insightfully portrayed as higher education's loss of the soul in its trajectory toward "established nonbelief." We believe that an attempt to reclaim and advance the Christian intellectual tradition is a first step toward helping churches, Christian organizations, and Christian institutions of higher education in the twenty-first century from following that same trajectory. It is to the exploration of this tradition that we now turn our attention.[1]

---

[1] See Carl F. H. Henry, *Confessions of a Theologian: An Autobiography* (Waco: Word, 1986); Douglas Sloan, *Faith and Knowledge* (Louisville: Westminster/John Knox, 1994); and also the June 2011 report from the Pew Forum on Religion and Public Life. In addition, please see T. S. Eliot, *Christianity and Culture* (New York: Harcourt Brace, 1940); and George M. Marsden, *The Soul of the American University: From Protestant Establishment to Established Nonbelief* (New York: Oxford University Press, 1994). Similar concepts can be found in Mark A. Noll, *The Scandal of the Evangelical Mind* (Grand Rapids, MI: Eerdmans, 1994); and his updated thoughts on these matters in *Jesus Christ and the Life of the Mind* (Grand Rapids, MI: Eerdmans, 2011). As we move forward with our observations regarding the development of these thoughts in the first two chapters of this volume, much of the material has been adapted from David S. Dockery, *Biblical Interpretation Then and Now* (Grand Rapids, MI: Baker, 1992).

APOSTOLIC GUIDANCE

The apostle Paul, writing to the church at Thessalonica, urged the followers of Jesus Christ to "stand firm and hold to the traditions that you were taught by us, either by our spoken word or by our letter" (2 Thess. 2:15). Similarly, the apostle exhorted Timothy, his apostolic legate, to "keep . . . the pattern of . . . teaching" (2 Tim. 1:13 NIV). The history of Christianity is best understood as a chain of memory. Our effort in this study guide and in this entire series is to introduce our readers to the great tradition of Christian thinking, which reflects the recognition that we need to reconnect aspects of that memory chain.

Wherever the Christian faith has been found, there has been a close association with the written Word of God, with books, education, and learning. Studying and interpreting the Bible became natural for members of the early Christian community, having inherited the practice from late Judaism. Virginia Stem Owens has suggested that studying literature developed from the practice of studying and interpreting the Bible:

> We in fact got the whole idea of literature as something to be taught and studied because we had already developed the habit with the Bible, the central text of Western civilization. At least ever since that category of teachers called rabbis sprang up in the Midrash, a collection of rabbinical commentary on the Hebrew scripture, we have been gnawing away at texts, chewing the gristle, sucking the marrow from the bones that are words.[2]

The Christian intellectual tradition has its roots in the interpretation of Holy Scripture. From the church's earliest days, Christians inherited the approaches to biblical interpretation found in the writings of both intertestamental Judaism and the contemporary Graeco-Roman world. From this dual heritage, there is an observable continuity with the hermeneutical methods

---

[2]Virginia Stem Owens, "Fiction and the Bible," *Reformed Journal* (July 1988): 12–15.

of the rabbis and Philo as well as of the followers of Plato and Aristotle. Yet, a discontinuity is also clearly evident as early Christianity established its own uniqueness by separating itself from Judaism and the surrounding Graeco-Roman religions.

BUILDING ON JEWISH TRADITION

Jewish interpreters, no matter how diverse their perspectives, found agreement on several points. First, they believed in the divine inspiration of Scripture. Second, they affirmed that the Torah contained the truth of God for the guidance of humanity. The biblical texts for the Jews of the first century were understood to be extremely rich in content and pregnant with plural meanings. Third, Jewish interpreters, because of their view that the biblical texts contained many meanings, considered both the plain or literal meaning and various implied meanings. Lastly, they maintained that the purpose of all interpretation involved translating the words of God into the lives of people, thus making them relevant for men and women in their own particular situations.

Building on these common commitments, the New Testament writers, by the use of numerous themes, images, and motifs, emphasized that the Scriptures find their fulfillment in Jesus Christ. The note of Philip's jubilant words, "We have found him" (John 1:45), was echoed by the Gospel writers as the way to interpret the Old Testament events, pictures, and ideas. The teachings of Jesus and the interpretive models of the apostles became the direct source for the trajectory that would become the Christian intellectual tradition.

THE BIBLE AS PRIMARY SOURCE FOR SHAPING THE CHRISTIAN TRADITION

From the earliest days of Christian history, Christians have used the Bible in various ways. This rich heritage has shaped the

Christian tradition in both individual and corporate practices. Some of these include:

1) the Bible as a source for information and understanding of life;
2) the Bible as a guide for worship;
3) the Bible as a wellspring to formulate Christian liturgy;
4) the Bible as a primary source for the formulation of theology;
5) the Bible as a text for preaching or teaching;
6) the Bible as a guide for pastoral care;
7) the Bible as the foundation for spiritual formation; and
8) the Bible as the model for literary and aesthetic enjoyment.

Beginning in the second century, some of these uses of the Bible started to shape the early stages of the Christian intellectual tradition, which was shaped by a shared faith in the uniqueness and significance of the life, death, and resurrection of Jesus of Nazareth.

LEARNING FROM THE APOSTOLIC FATHERS, THE SCHOOLS OF ALEXANDRIA AND ANTIOCH

At the close of the apostolic age, some marked changes began to occur. Primarily, the New Testament books were in the process of being recognized as Scripture. The relation of the New Testament to the Old Testament was a key question for the church in the second and third centuries. Marcion (ca. 85–160) and the Gnostics abandoned the Old Testament as a Christian book and re-created certain New Testament texts to suit themselves. Orthodox Christian leaders at this time focused on the need to counter the Gnostic proposal that the God of the Old Testament was incompatible with the God revealed in the New Testament. As texts were challenged, altered, and even abandoned, the church had to demonstrate on biblical grounds that the same God was revealed in both Testaments and that, therefore, the church should not abandon the Old Testament. We will amplify the church's response to Marcion in chapter 3.

The church's preaching understood the Old Testament Scripture in terms of the incarnation of Jesus Christ. This was evidenced in both the early Christians' attitude toward and reading of the Old Testament. They regarded the law and the prophets as well as the events and worship of Israel as part of the Christian tradition because they believed that these all testified to Jesus Christ. Paul, for example, in 1 Corinthians 15:3–4, insisted that everything regarding Christ took place "in accordance with the Scriptures."

In many ways, the beginnings of the Christian intellectual tradition can be traced to the conversation between Philip and the Ethiopian, recorded in Acts 8. In the role of teacher, Philip asked the Ethiopian, "Do you understand what you are reading?" (v. 30). We hear this answer in verse 31: "How can I, unless someone guides me?" For nearly two thousand years, the search for understanding and guidance and the resulting explanations have continued in an ongoing conversation among the saints, represented by first-century Christ followers, third-century Neoplatonist thinkers, fourth-century theologians wrestling with the meaning of the Holy Trinity, eighth-century Irish missionaries, thirteenth-century Schoolmen, sixteenth-century Reformers, eighteenth-century pastor-theologian-philosophers, and twenty-first-century believers in the southern hemisphere. While diverse voices and varied emphases have obviously been offered, the conversation has continued with the hope of better articulating the confession of "one Lord," and "one faith" described by the apostle Paul in Ephesians 4:5.

As the church moved into the second century, following the death of the apostles, greater attention was given to the moral and ethical instruction of believers. As a result, what might be called a rather functional and practical reading of Scripture came to characterize the works of Clement of Rome (d. ca. 100) and Ignatius (d. ca. 117). Apart from the *Didache* (ca. 100–120), which was a teaching manual, and the *Shepherd of Hermas* (ca. 120–150), which was more apocalyptic, the majority of works in the early decades of the second century were quite practical in their orientation.

During the latter half of the second century, the rise of heresies became so widespread that they provoked in the church at large a response that was to be of enormous significance for the history of Christian thought. The challenges involved: (1) a need to answer the Gnostics, demonstrating the continuity between the Testaments; (2) a need to answer the Montanists by showing the development, as well as the cessation, of revelation; and (3) a need to convince the Judaizers within Christianity, as well as Judaism in general, of the discontinuity of the two Testaments. The primary responses were the philosophical approaches of Justin Martyr (d. 165) and the more theological perspectives of Irenaeus (d. ca. 202) and Tertullian (d. ca. 220).

JUSTIN MARTYR

For Justin Martyr, both general and special revelation were the outgrowth of the *Logos*. Pagan philosophers, he claimed, possessed some aspect of the *Logos*, but Jesus was and is the true *Logos*, and the Bible contains the written residue of the *Logos*. Justin brilliantly linked the Old Testament to the New, the very antithesis of both Judaism and Marcionism, or what some refer to as Marcionite Gnosticism. Marcion's total rejection of the Old Testament was the exact opposite of Justin's commitment to the continuity of the Testaments. Drawing on the messianic prophecies from the Jewish tradition, Justin argued that Jesus clearly was the expected Messiah who fulfilled all of the Old Testament Scriptures literally or typologically. Thus Justin established his apologetic method on proof from prophecy. His writings, primarily his *Dialogue with Trypho*, served as a gold mine of information on second-century Christianity. In the *Dialogue*, Justin described his philosophical pilgrimage. He first attached himself to a stoic philosopher, and then he studied with a shrewd Peripatetic. He later followed a celebrated Pythagorean, and finally he became a Platonist.[3]

It should be noted that Justin did not consider his turn to Christianity to be merely a next step in his journey. Justin did not just use Greek philosophy; he passed judgment on it. Only if the philosophical teaching was found to be in accord with Christian teaching did Justin acknowledge the philosophy as true.[4] The *Dialogue* shows how Justin developed a Christian apologetic faithful to the early Christian creed or confession commonly referred to as "the rule of faith" (something similar to the Apostles' Creed), how he engaged the philosophers of his day, and how he interpreted the biblical texts. Since the time of Justin, the dialogue between faith and reason, between faith and culture, has reflected two essential characteristics of the Christian intellectual heritage: (1) faith seeks understanding; and (2) intellectual inquiry invites a response of faith.

IRENAEUS AND TERTULLIAN

The church's estimate of its theological norms underwent certain adjustments in the final decades of the second century. The distinction between Scripture and the church's living tradition, as coordinated instruments in conveying the apostolic testimony, became more clearly appreciated, and a growing importance, if not a primacy, began to be attached to the latter.[5] This development resulted from the great struggle between orthodoxy and the Gnostic heretics. This developing, more mature position was exemplified, with minor differences, in the writings of Irenaeus

---

[3]Robert M. Grant, "Aristotle and the Conversion of Justin," *Journal of Theological Studies* 7 (1956): 246–48; Oscar S. Karsaune, "The Conversion of Justin Martyr," *Studia Theologica* 30 (1976): 53–74.

[4]So claimed Henry Chadwick, *Early Christian Thought and the Classical Tradition* (Oxford: Clarendon, 1966), 20; Robert Wilken, "Toward a Social Interpretation of Early Christian Apologetics," *Church History* 39 (1970): 437–58.

[5]See J. N. D. Kelly, *Early Christian Doctrines*, 4th rev. ed. (San Francisco: Harper & Row, 1978), 35–41.

and Tertullian at the end of the second century. Rowan A. Greer has incisively and helpfully summarized this period:

1) A Christian Bible was the product of the formative period of early Christianity (30–180). Before Irenaeus, we find the church struggling to define its Scriptures and to come to terms with their interpretation, but it was only by the end of the second century that the diversity of earliest Christianity had yielded to an ecumenical unity. The emergence of a Christian Bible became a central feature of that unity.

2) Basic to the task of the formative period was the transformation of the Hebrew Scriptures so that they served as a witness to Christ.

3) With Irenaeus we find the first clear evidence of a Christian Bible and also a framework of interpretation in what is often referred to as the church's rule of faith. The rule of faith, as a kind of creed or confessional statement, outlined the theological story that found its focus in the incarnate Lord.[6]

The authority of the church, the canon, and the church's faith had reached new heights by the beginning of the third century, but the inroads of Christian creativity were in infantile stages. We now turn to the creative genius of the Alexandrians, particularly the work of Origen (185–254). The third century saw the rise of schools, intertwined with classical learning, science, philosophy, and centers of art. The Christian intellectual tradition shaped by serious biblical interpretation began to develop and mature in the Schools of Alexandria and Antioch.

THE ALEXANDRIANS

Origen, born in Egypt, studied under Clement (ca. 150–215) in the School of Alexandria. He followed Clement, who will receive attention in chapter 5, as the leader and primary teacher in this

---

[6]James L. Kugel and Rowan A. Greer, *Early Biblical Interpretation* (Philadelphia: Westminster, 1986), 111–12.

school, a position he held for twenty-eight years while pursuing an ascetic and extremely pious life.

Origen's teaching reflected his love for and nurture of the individual Christians under his care. Origen's work was greatly influenced by the Neoplatonist thought he had learned from the father of Neoplatonic philosophy, Ammonius Saccus. Ultimately, Origen was a churchman who lived with the tension of his Neoplatonist philosophy, his creative biblical interpretation, and his commitment to the church's rule of faith. Origen maintained that biblical interpretation, theological formation, and philosophical engagement must be understood according to the rule of faith, which probably included the following items:

1) *A doctrine of God.* There is one God, the Father, who created the universe and governs it by providence. Worship is due to God alone, who gave the law to the Jews and sent his son Jesus Christ to redeem the world.

2) *A doctrine of Christ.* Jesus Christ, the Messiah whom the Old Testament foretold, was a man born of Mary, who as a virgin miraculously conceived him. In Palestine Jesus taught and performed miracles, was crucified under Pontius Pilate, died, and was buried. He descended into hell to liberate the righteous dead. He rose from the dead, appeared to his disciples, and ascended into heaven, where he reigns with God the Father. Christ will return to judge the living and the newly resurrected dead. Jesus Christ is divine and hence worthy of worship but not identical with God the Father.

3) *A doctrine of the Spirit.* God's Spirit inspired the prophets and apostles who wrote the Bible and continues to enliven believers.

4) *A doctrine of spiritual beings.* There are rational beings not confined, as we are, to earthly bodies. Some are angels who worship God and carry out God's commands. Others are demons—probably fallen angels—who follow the commands of Satan, their prince. The demons disguise themselves as gods, thereby deceiving the pagans into sustaining them with sacrifices, even as they seek to entice believers into heresy and sin.

5) *A doctrine of last things.* At the end of time, God will destroy
the world he made. When this happens all the dead will resume
their bodies, and Christ will then welcome the righteous into
everlasting happiness and condemn the wicked, along with
Satan and the demons, to everlasting torment.[7]

Origen's version of the rule of faith provided the third-century church with a response to the heterodox proposals from
Marcion and the Gnostics. As Albert Outler has noted, Origen
attempted deliberately in his articulation of the rule of faith to
sum up all doctrinal points on which there was general agreement
in the church.[8] Origen clearly distinguished between what he designated as "necessary" doctrines, which the apostles "delivered"
in plainest terms to all believers, and other doctrines. These necessary doctrines corresponded to the threefold baptismal formula
of Matthew 28. Within Origen's discussion of these doctrines can
be found all that is essential to the rule of faith as defined by the
usage of Irenaeus, Tertullian, and Clement of Alexandria, and
which even had traces in *1 Clement* (often referred to as Clement
of Rome).

In *1 Clement*, however, the essentials of the rule of faith were
not as systematized as in Origen's preface to *First Principles*. An
obvious development and expansion of both the Christian intellectual tradition and the church's doctrinal expression took place
between the time of *1 Clement* and Origen. The emergence of
Marcion and succeeding Gnostics can account for this development as the church responded more vigorously with each generation to the challenges raised against Christian orthodoxy. We will
explore these challenges in more detail in chapter 3.

---

[7]See Joseph Wilson Trigg, *The Bible and Philosophy in the Third Century* (Atlanta: John Knox, 1983), 13–14.
[8]See Albert C. Outler, "Origen and the *Regula Fidei*," *Church History* 8 (1939): 212–21; see also P. M. O'Clerigh, "The Meaning of Dogma in Origen," in *Jewish and Christian Self-Definition, I: The Shaping of Christianity in the Second and Third Centuries*, ed. J. Sanders (Philadelphia: Fortress, 1980), 201–16; and H. E. W. Turner, *The Patristic Doctrine of Redemption: A Study of the Development of Doctrine During the First Five Centuries* (London: Mowbray, 1952).

The challenges to the rule of faith in the fourth century needed a more solid solution than the creative legacy of Origen could fully provide. Because the Gnostic systems made Christ an intermediary rather than a creator, thus something less than God and still different from humanity, the rule of faith had to be expounded more clearly. By the end of the third century, the issues needed further definition and clarification.[9] The biblical realism of this period tended to accentuate the historical and human aspects of Jesus, though his heavenly origin was not denied.[10]

During this time Arius (d. 336) attempted to maintain monotheism by asserting that Jesus, as God's Son, was lower than God the Father and indeed owed his existence to the Father's decision to produce the created order. This led to the Arian controversy, in which John 14:28, "The Father is greater than I," became a battleground text. Arianism was condemned at the Council of Nicaea (325), but the controversy continued into the next century until the Council of Chalcedon (451).[11]

It was Athanasius (296–373), the leading opponent of Arius, who argued that theological talk about the nature of God could proceed only by the way of analogy. The crux of the debate focused around the description of Jesus as *homoousios* (meaning "of one nature or substance"), which allowed a proper differentiation between Jesus and the Father without necessitating an Arian subordinationism. The Arians had alternatively suggested *homoiousios* (meaning "of a similar nature or substance").

Arianism was declared heretical at the Council of Nicaea, with Athanasius defending his orthodox view by appealing to

---

[9]See Aloys Grillmeier, *Christ in Christian Tradition, vol. 1: From the Apostolic Age to Chalcedon (451)*, trans. John Bowden, 2nd ed. (Atlanta: John Knox, 1974), 167–80.

[10]See R. V. Sellers, *Two Ancient Christologies: A Study in the Christological Thought of the Schools of Alexandria and Antioch in the Early History of Christian Doctrine* (London: SPCK, 1954), who notes that the two schools could not see they were contending for the same theological principles. What divided them was their philosophical and ecclesiastical differences.

[11]See the informative discussion in Gerald L. Bray, *Creeds, Councils, and Christ* (Downers Grove, IL: InterVarsity, 1984), 92–171.

the theological meaning of Scripture. Athanasius supported the idea of "one substance" (*homoousios*) as conveyed in Scripture in John 1:18; 6:46; 8:42; 10:30; and 14:10, even though the specific word, *homoousios*, is not found in Scripture.[12] The tensions of the fourth-century debates created opportunities for philosophical influences, which at times overshadowed and influenced the interpretation of Scripture. But as R. P. C. Hanson has concluded, "It is hard to deny that the doctrine of Athanasius was more faithful to the New Testament account of the significance of Jesus Christ than that of the Arians, whose fundamental trouble, one suspects, was that they could not believe that God really has communicated himself in Christ."[13]

The writings of Athanasius have come to be regarded as the essential and definitive statements on the key Christological controversies of the time. Athanasius shaped the church's understanding of the expanding rule of faith, which became the framework for the developing Christian intellectual tradition. The brilliant fourth-century theologian greatly influenced the three great Cappadocian fathers: Basil of Caesarea (ca. 329–379), his friend Gregory of Nazianzus (ca. 330–389), and his brother Gregory of Nyssa (ca. 330–395). In this splendid trio, orthodox statements about Jesus Christ and the Trinitarian God reached their climax. Because of the Christological debates in the fourth and fifth centuries, church leaders became more theologically oriented in their approach to reading Scripture. The consistent articulation of the church's orthodox faith, coupled with pastoral concerns for the edification of the faithful, provided norms for the shaping and advancement of the Christian intellectual tradition.

---

[12]See Craig A. Blaising, *Athanasius* (Lanham, MD: University Press, 1992); David F. Wells, *The Person of Christ* (Wheaton, IL: Crossway, 1984), 98–109; Peter J. Leithart, *Athanasius* (Grand Rapids, MI: Baker, 2011).

[13]R. P. C. Hanson, "Biblical Exegesis in the Early Church," *Cambridge History of the Bible*, vol. 1, ed. P. R. Ackroyd and C. F. Evans (Cambridge, UK: Cambridge University Press, 1970), 1:453; see Johannes Quasten, *Patrology*, 4 vols. (repr. Westminster, MD: Christian Classics, 1984), 3:37–39.

THE ANTIOCHENES: AN IMPORTANT
ADVANCEMENT IN BIBLICAL INTERPRETATION

In order to describe the work of the School of Antioch in biblical interpretation, we will concentrate on Theodore of Mopsuestia (ca. 350–428) and John Chrysostom (354–407), particularly the influence of Aristotelian thought and the place of typological interpretation in their approach to reading the Bible. While it can certainly be said that all Christian theology during this period was based on the interpretation of Scripture, especially was this the case for Theodore.[14]

Theodore's method of biblical interpretation was the purest representation of Antiochene hermeneutics. Theodore was the first to treat the Psalms historically and systematically while treating the Gospel narratives factually, paying attention to the particulars of transition and to the minutiae of grammar and punctuation. His approach can be described as "anti-allegorical," rejecting interpretations that denied the historical reality of what the scriptural text affirmed. Instead of an allegorical approach, Theodore and the Antiochenes, as Rowan A. Greer has suggested, preferred typological interpretation as the normative method for understanding the Old Testament texts.[15]

The great value of allegorical interpretation for the Alexandrians was that it made possible a theologically unified interpretation of the Bible as a whole. Theodore, attempting to present a unified theological exposition, viewed the Bible as a record of the historical development of the divine redemptive plan. Ultimately, this history must be understood from the perspective of the overall purposes of God to provide the setting of God's gracious act in Christ Jesus, by which the new age of salvation was realized. Theodore, the dedicated interpreter and teacher, was joined in his efforts by the gifted preacher John Chrysostom.

---

[14]See J. N. D. Kelly, *Early Christian Doctrines*, 76–77.
[15]See Rowan A. Greer, *Theodore of Mopsuestia* (London: Faith, 1961), 94.

John Chrysostom gave primary attention to the literal, grammatical, and historical interpretation of Scripture. Like others in the Antiochene tradition, he was influenced by Aristotelian philosophy. Aristotle seemed more down to earth when compared to Plato's more other-worldly views. Chrysostom, more than his Alexandrian predecessors, was aware of the human factor in Scripture and sought to do justice to the dual authorship of biblical revelation. Yet, he maintained that the Bible spoke with a unified voice.

Chrysostom, like Theodore and other Antiochene representatives, emphasized the historical meaning of the biblical text. While never articulating his approach in these words, it seems he was attempting to discover the intended meaning of the biblical author. Chrysostom rejected crudely literal interpretations of the Bible from both the Antiochene laity and the criticisms of the Alexandrians. He was cautious that no figurative expression in the Bible be misunderstood from either a too literal or a too fanciful interpretation.[16]

For Chrysostom, theology and hermeneutics were not theoretical exercises, but practical and pastoral. It is generally true that the Alexandrians looked for both a literal and allegorical meaning in Scripture, and the Antiochenes found a more historical and typological sense. The Alexandrians looked to the rule of faith, mystical interpretation, and authority as sources for shaping the Christian intellectual tradition. The Antiochenes looked to reason and historical development of Scripture as the focus for understanding Christian thought. These approaches set the stage for the widely influential and shaping work of Augustine.

---

[16]See Stephen Neill, *Chrysostom and His Message* (New York: Association, 1963); Chrysostomus Baur, *John Chrysostom and His Time*, trans. M. Gonzaga, 2 vols. (Westminster, MD: Newman, 1959); and Jaroslav Pelikan, *The Preaching of Chrysostom* (Philadelphia: Fortress, 1967).

2

THE DEVELOPMENT OF THE GREAT TRADITION

A student at a Christian university who has not encountered the
proposal of the Christian intellectual tradition—from Paul to
Augustine, from Irenaeus to Dante, Aquinas, Luther, Milton,
and moderns such as Lewis and Polanyi, along with those who have
challenged and now challenge that tradition—such a student has been
grievously shortchanged in his or her University education. This is
true for students majoring in theology, philosophy, or the liberal
arts. It is true, to varying levels of intensity, for all students. If, that is,
the Christian in the claim to be a Christian University refers to governing
conviction and not merely to a hangover of historical accident.

Richard John Neuhaus, "A University of a Particular Kind," *First Things* (2007)

The emphasis on biblical interpretation as foundational for serious Christian thought and engagement was important not only
for the Antiochenes but also for the greatest doctors of the church,
Jerome (ca. 341–420) and Augustine (354–430). Jerome was a
more able linguist and translator than any of his colleagues in the
early church. His eclectic model for interpreting Scripture com-
bined what was best in both the Alexandrian and Antiochene
Schools. Without question Jerome ranks as a biblical interpreter
of the first order, a reputation that endures even to this day.[1]
Yet, it was Augustine who advanced Christian thinking in most
significant ways.

---

[1]See J. N. D. Kelly, *Jerome: His Life, Writings, and Controversies* (London: Duckworth, 1975).

AUGUSTINE: THE FATHER OF THE CHRISTIAN INTELLECTUAL TRADITION

For Protestants, Augustine serves as the dominant figure in the history of Christian thought and biblical interpretation between the time of the apostles and the sixteenth-century Reformation. For Roman Catholics, Augustine's influence during this period is rivaled only by that of Thomas Aquinas (1225–1274). In the history of philosophy, Augustine is only slightly less important; he was the most influential philosopher between Plotinus, in the third century, and Aquinas. In this regard, Augustine's work has shaped the best of the Christian intellectual tradition like few others during the two-thousand-year history of the church.

Augustine's life serves as an important key to understanding his thought. As described in his *Confessions*, Augustine in his youth seldom lost an opportunity to pursue one sin or another.[2] He took a mistress when he was seventeen and fathered an illegitimate son before he was twenty. About the same time, he began a relationship with a dualistic religious and philosophical system known as Manichaeism, which taught that two principles—Light and Dark, God and Matter—are eternal. Augustine claimed that Manichaeism appealed to him intellectually because it appeared to offer a superior answer to the problem of evil than what he had discovered in his mother's Christianity. Also, Manichaeism made fewer moral demands upon him. When he gradually realized through the study of the liberal arts, particularly philosophy, the inconsistency of the religion of Mani, Augustine did not take up with this movement or any other religion, "because they were

---

[2]See Augustine, *Confessions: The Odyssey of Soul* (Cambridge, UK: Cambridge University Press, 1969). The *Confessions* are divided into two parts: the first part (chaps. 1–9) describes Augustine up to the time of his conversion and the death of his influential Christian mother, Monica; the second part (chaps. 10–13), added at a later date, describes Augustine's thoughts during the time of the writings. The unity of the work is to be found in the central theme of the praise of God "for the good things and for the bad," and in the autobiographical aspect, which was also present in the second part. The *Confessions* were begun after April 4, 397 (the death of Ambrose) and completed around 400. See the helpful discussion in A. Pincherle, "The 'Confessions' of St. Augustine," *Augustinian Studies* 7 (1976): 119–33.

without the saving name of Christ."[3] Instead, he fell into the temptation of skepticism, with academics at the helm of his life.

The road to his conversion began at Milan with the preaching of Ambrose (ca. 339–397), which dispersed the Manichaean difficulties and provided the key for the interpretation of the Old Testament with the use of allegorical hermeneutics. Under the influence of Ambrose, Augustine's difficulties about the Bible began to be resolved, and the process was accelerated by the discovery of Neoplatonist philosophy, in which he could find confirmation of much that he found in the Gospel of John.

Augustine's conversion took place in AD 386, at which time he authored *Against the Skeptics*. He was appointed as coadjutor bishop and was consecrated as bishop of Hippo Regius in 395. His numerous writings included polemical works against the Manichaeans, the Donatists, and the Pelagians, in addition to significantly important theological works such as *The Trinity* and *The City of God*. During this time a steady stream of biblical commentaries also flowed from his pen.

Augustine was among the first to recognize the importance of one's presuppositions when interpreting Holy Scripture. He was perhaps the greatest of the Christian Platonists. The integration of biblical data and Platonic philosophy can be seen in Augustine's famous maxim: *Credo ut intelligam* (I believe in order that I may understand). Augustine derived the biblical foundation of this principle from the Latin version of Isaiah 7:9 (Unless you believe, you shall not understand) and from the Platonic notion of innate first principles.

Long before the insights of contemporary semiotics or semantics, Augustine recognized that things in the created world could function as signs or symbols through which God was understood. Understanding is possible because of the illumination afforded by the uncreated light of God. Augustine believed that for the mind

---

[3]Augustine, *Confessions*, 5.15.24.

to see God, it must be illumined by God, and this results in: (1) a faith that believes that what we look for, when seen, ought to make us blessed; (2) a hope that is assured that vision will follow right looking; and (3) a love which longs to see and enjoy.[4]

The goal of biblical interpretation should prioritize the love of God and neighbor (see Matt. 22:37–39), the ordering of the Christian life toward its heavenly home. Augustine's reading of Holy Scripture emphasized the canonical meaning of a text within the context of the entire biblical canon, the priority of faith, the significance of signs, the goal of love, and both the historical and allegorical meanings. He did not limit the Scripture to just one sense; when he approached the Bible, he tended to prioritize theological issues over historical ones.[5]

Similar to Jerome, in the course of his theological development, Augustine began to emphasize more strongly the literal and historical sense of Scripture, though, for Augustine, the theological was always primary. From this framework, Augustine not only became the most articulate advocate for the Christian intellectual tradition but advanced it as had no one before him. In doing so, he gladly upheld the authority of the rule of faith thus shaping the confessional tradition that we will explore in chapter 4. Excesses in Augustine's interpretation or theologizing were thereby modified by his concern for a catholic interpretation of Scripture, faithful to the authority of both church and creed.[6] Thus Augustine's genius could hold together creativity and creed; author, text, and interpreter; the historical and the figurative/allegorical, as well as faith and reason.

In holding together faith and reason, Augustine provided

---

[4]See Belford D. Jackson, "Semantics and Hermeneutics in Saint Augustine's *De doctrina Christiana*," PhD diss., Yale University, 1967, 171–87; also Bernard Ramm, *Protestant Biblical Interpretation*, 3rd rev. ed. (Grand Rapids, MI: Baker, 1970), 34–35.

[5]See Beryl Smalley, *The Study of the Bible in the Middle Ages*, 2nd ed. (Oxford: Blackwell, 1952), 22–24.

[6]See ibid.; G. R. Evans, *The Language and Logic of the Bible: The Earlier Middle Ages* (Cambridge, UK: Cambridge University Press, 1984); G. W. H. Lampe, ed., *The Cambridge History of the Bible 2: The West from the Fathers to the Reformation* (Cambridge, UK: Cambridge University Press, 1969).

a model for thinking Christianly about the world, stressing the priority of faith for understanding God's revelation to humanity in creation and experience and ultimately in Jesus Christ and Holy Scripture. In doing so, Augustine always stressed that biblical interpretation and Christian thinking about all aspects of life should encourage love for God, for the church, and for neighbor. Augustine's influence on the shape of the Christian intellectual tradition has been, in many ways, incalculable. Some would even suggest that the contributions to this tradition over the past fifteen hundred years are best understood as a footnote to the work of Augustine.

THE MEDIEVAL TRADITION: FROM AUGUSTINE TO AQUINAS

The seven great ecumenical councils of the church (325–787) took place during turbulent times. As the church expanded and matured, it also faced new and greater challenges concerning the church's beliefs. How should the Trinity be believed and proclaimed? If Jesus Christ is fully God, how can he simultaneously be fully human? If Jesus Christ is one person, how do we understand his two natures and two wills? What is meant by the phrase "the Holy Spirit, the lifegiver"? Questions regarding the Trinity, the incarnation of Jesus Christ, and the nature and sinfulness of humanity ushered in and characterized the years known as the medieval period. These were years during which the barbarians were chipping away at the borders of the Roman Empire, conquering large portions of it. Also, it was a time when the church's understandings of its leadership and organization were developing into their hierarchical form. The Christian intellectual tradition during this time was challenged, expanded, and strengthened, particularly through the work of Anselm, Bernard of Clairvaux, and Thomas Aquinas.

Anselm (1033–1109) served as archbishop of Canterbury

from 1093 to 1109. In his book *Proslogion*, Anselm, through the use of reason, made a case for the existence of God through what is known as the ontological argument. He argued that since God nothing greater than God can be conceived, there must be a supreme being. Therefore, because humans can conceive of God, God must exist. If he did not exist, he would not be the greatest conceivable being. Since men and women can think of God, it is implied that there must be a God. Anselm's contribution to the Christian intellectual tradition was his attempt to show that men and women were capable of using reason to explore the things of God. Anselm appealed to Scripture and to tradition, but his efforts attempted to bring together the roles of reason and faith.

Bernard of Clairvaux (1090–1153) was a faithful Cistercian who built a major Cistercian center in Clairvaux. One of the most significant leaders in the twelfth century, Bernard was a popular preacher and an author of important works on Scripture and monasticism. While known for his devotional spirit, Bernard faithfully extended the work of the early church tradition to the extent that he was sometimes called the "last of the church fathers." Yet, he was capable of serious apologetic work, using reason and brilliant argumentation at the Council of Sens in 1140 to refute the false teaching of Abelard on the atonement of Christ. Like Anselm, Bernard brought together Scripture, tradition, and reason in the practice of engaged and engaging Christian thinking.[7]

Thomas Aquinas (1225–1274), the greatest thinker in the medieval period, reframed much of Augustinian thought in an Aristotelian perspective. Aquinas is now regarded as one of the most important teachers in the Roman Catholic tradition. Employing Aristotelian thought, he, like Anselm and Bernard before him, tried to harmonize reason and faith. Similar to Anselm, Thomas adopted a methodology of setting up contradictory

---

[7]See James Houston's introduction to Bernard of Clairvaux, *The Love of God and Spiritual Friendship*, ed. James Houston (Portland, OR: Multnomah, 1983); also William C. Placher, *A History of Christian Theology* (Philadelphia: Westminster, 1983), 146–48.

statements about an issue, seeking to find a solution through use of reason. His most important works, among many from his pen, were *Summa Theologiae* and *Summa contra Gentiles*.[8]

The prominent place of reason in the thought of Thomas should not lead one to think he downplayed the role of Scripture. On the contrary, Thomas sought to demonstrate that the spiritual sense of Scripture was always based on the literal sense and derived from it.[9] He also suggested that the literal sense of the biblical text should be equated with the meaning intended by the biblical author. The medieval exegetes and theologians admitted that the words of Scripture contained a meaning in the historical situation in which they were first uttered, but overall these scholars denied that the final and full meaning of those words were restricted to what the initial audience heard or understood.

Nowhere is serious Christian engagement better seen in this medieval period than in the work of Thomas Aquinas. Aquinas carried on a multi-sided conversation with the biblical text, the church fathers, and Aristotle. Simultaneously he invested in both dialogical and apologetical responses to Muslim and Jewish thinkers such as Averroes and Maimonides. Before and after the Reformation, the work of Aquinas greatly influenced Roman Catholic thinkers as well as Protestant philosophers.

The medieval period saw the development of some of the first great universities. These institutions were largely established for the purposes of professional education, with some general education for the elite. Of the seventy-nine universities in existence in Europe during this time, Salerno was best known for medicine, Bologna for law, and Paris for theology. Established within medieval Christendom, where the Christian faith provided shape and illumination for the intellectual landscape, the central mission of

---

[8]See E. Gilson, *The Christian Philosophy of St. Thomas Aquinas*, trans. L. K. Shook (London: Victor Gollanez, 1957).

[9]See Thomas Aquinas, *On Interpretation*, trans. J. T. Osterle (Milwaukee: Marquette University Press, 1962).

the university generally focused on inquiry in pursuit of truth. Faith in the context of medieval Christendom was understood to be an indispensable ally, not an enemy, of reason and intellectual exploration.[10] Since the medieval period, Christian universities, which arose *ex corde ecclesiae,* from the "heart of the church," have been one of the primary places where the Christian tradition has been advanced.

RENAISSANCE AND REFORMATION: ERASMUS, LUTHER, AND CALVIN

Martin Luther (1483–1546), the great Reformer, started his career as a biblical interpreter by employing the allegorical method but later abandoned it.[11] While Luther is widely recognized as the father of the Reformation, in reality, he, in many ways, carried forward the work of Peter Waldo (1140–1218), John Wycliffe (1330–1384), Jon Hus (1373–1415), Girolamo Savonarola (1452–1498), and even Desiderius Erasmus (1466–1536). All of these prioritized the Scriptures in bold ways, but it was Erasmus, even more so than Luther, through the influence of John Colet (1466–1519), who rediscovered the priority of the historical sense of biblical interpretation.[12] Erasmus exemplified the finest in Renaissance scholarship, which emphasized the priority of the original sources (*ad fontes*). The ultimate source to which Erasmus turned was the Greek New Testament. Coupled with his emphasis on the sources was a truly historical understanding of ancient texts, yet he also

---

[10]See Mark Noll, "Reconsidering Christendom," in *The Future of Christian Learning*, ed. Thomas A. Howard (Grand Rapids, MI: Brazos, 2008), 23–70; also Alister McGrath, *The Intellectual Origins of the European Reformation* (Oxford: Blackwell, 1987, 2004), 11–117.

[11]See Raymond Barry Skelton, "Martin Luther's Concept of Biblical Interpretation in Historical Perspective," PhD diss., Fuller Theological Seminary, 1974; also Jaroslav Pelikan, *Luther the Expositor* (St. Louis, MO: Concordia, 1959); David S. Dockery, "The Christological Hermeneutics of Martin Luther," in *Grace Theological Journal* 4 (1983): 189–203.

[12]See A. Rabil, *Erasmus and the New Testament: The Mind of a Christian Humanist* (San Antonio: Trinity University Press, 1972); J. H. Bentley, *Humanist and Holy Writ* (Princeton, NJ: Princeton University Press, 1983); J. W. Aldridge, *The Hermeneutics of Erasmus* (Richmond, VA: John Knox, 1966); David S. Dockery, "The Foundation of Reformation Hermeneutics: A Fresh Look at Erasmus," in *Evangelical Hermeneutics*, ed. Michael Bauman and David Hall (Camp Hill, PA: Christian Publications, 1995), 53–76.

desired for the biblical texts to bring edification to the readers through the spiritual sense.

As significant and innovative as was the work of Erasmus, the pivotal and shaping figures of the Reformation were Martin Luther (1483–1546) and John Calvin (1509–1564).[13] Luther gave new focus to the Christian intellectual tradition with his use of a Christological method of biblical interpretation, which shaped his engagement with church, culture, and society. Martin Luther broke the stronghold of fanciful interpretation with his commitment to *sola scriptura*, which stressed not only the primacy of Scripture but also the historical sense of Scripture as the true and only sense that provides a sound framework for thinking Christianly about God and his world.

Luther, reclaiming the key aspects of the Augustinian tradition, also insisted that the Bible itself is its own best interpreter. These commitments rested on the foundation of a complete trust in the Bible's truthfulness and authority. Believing that the God of truth had spoken in Scripture, Luther likewise believed that humans must stand under the authority of the Bible. Scripture provided the framework for seeing all of life and for understanding all human thinking, because, for Luther, the Bible is the very Word of God itself.

Luther thought deeply about the relationship between faith and reason, demanding that the human intellect adjust itself to the teachings of Holy Scripture. Reason can certainly be used to discern truth and to explore intellectual pursuits, but it cannot be used to judge the truth value of Scripture. Not unlike other great thinkers, Luther's theory was often more consistent than his practice in this regard. Yet, even with such inconsistencies, Luther stands as a model for others in insisting that all Christian thinking be brought in line with the Bible rather than the other way around.[14]

---

[13]See Timothy George, *Theology of the Reformers* (Nashville: Broadman, 1988).
[14]See A. S. Wood, *Luther's Principles of Biblical Interpretation* (London: Tyndale, 1960).

Luther's bold advances have influenced Christian thinkers for five centuries, yet it was John Calvin who, in a sense, "out-Luthered" Luther to shape aspects of the Christian intellectual tradition that have developed since the sixteenth century.

John Calvin was the finest interpreter of Scripture and the most precise Christian thinker of this period. Even a rival like Jacob Arminius claimed that Calvin's work was incomparable, saying, "He stands above others, above most, indeed, above all."[15] In 1536, at the age of only twenty-six, Calvin published the first edition of his *Institutes of the Christian Religion.* The final edition, revised in 1559, was nearly three times the size of the original. Calvin stressed education, providing a catechetical system that has been carried all over the world. Calvin's theology influenced large sectors of Europe, Old and New England. He wrote commentaries on almost every book of the Bible. Above all, Calvin appealed to the witness of the Holy Spirit as a guide for understanding both God's natural and special revelation. Maintaining that the testimony of the Holy Spirit was more important than all reason, Calvin insisted that it was the inward testimony of the Spirit that connected a person's heart and mind to the Word of God. While certainly not rejecting the role of reason, Calvin believed that human minds were tainted by sin and the impact of the fall. Thus, Calvin consistently appealed to the illumination of the Spirit above human judgment. Luther, Calvin, along with Ulrich Zwingli (1484–1531), and other Reformation and Post-Reformation thinkers, contended that the Scripture must be believed, rightly interpreted, applied, and experienced to truly and redemptively advance the Christian intellectual tradition.[16]

---

[15]Cited by C. Bangs, *Arminius: A Study in the Dutch Reformation* (Nashville: Abingdon, 1921) 287–88.

[16]See P. A. Verhoef, "Luther and Calvin's Exegetical Library," *Concordian Theological Journal* 3 (1968): 5–20; B. A. Gerrish, *The Old Protestantism and the New: Essays on the Reformation Heritage* (Chicago: University of Chicago Press, 1982).

POST-REFORMATION AND MODERN THOUGHT: FROM THE WEST TO THE GLOBAL SOUTH

To focus on the Christian intellectual tradition during the church's first sixteen centuries leads us to an emphasis upon the various streams that we have highlighted: Alexandrian, Antiochene, Augustinian, East and West, Thomistic, Lutheran, Calvinistic, and others. Beginning with the seventeenth century, as these streams proliferated, it frankly became even more difficult to speak of a single tradition. From these various movements a concern soon arose regarding the growing fragmentation of the great tradition. Philipp Melanchthon (1497–1560) and others began to raise questions about this proliferating fragmentation that they were observing. Fresh calls for unity were issued, reminding others of their shared confession around the Nicene Creed: "We believe the church is one, holy, catholic, and apostolic." But the various forms of the Christian tradition seemed only to expand.[17]

Many aspects of the expansion were good and hopeful as the Christian message began more and more to influence all sectors of life, even as the Christian message circled the globe. On the other hand, the vast influence of Enlightenment and post-Enlightenment thought challenged the very heart of the Christian intellectual tradition, raising questions about authority, tradition, and the role of reason. The Enlightenment, which blossomed in the eighteenth century, was a watershed in the history of Western civilization. The Christian consensus that had existed from the fourth through the sixteenth centuries was hampered, if not broken, by a radical secular spirit. The Enlightenment philosophy could be characterized by its stress on the primacy of nature and reason over special revelation. Along with this elevated view of reason, the movement

---

[17]See the discussion of the various streams that began to develop at this important moment in the Christian movement in David S. Dockery, "So Many Denominations," *Southern Baptists, Evangelicals, and the Future of Denominationalism* (Nashville: Broadman, 2011). Also, see the work by Richard Gamble, *The Great Tradition* (Wilmington, DE: ISI Books, 2007), which is instructive and helpful.

reflected a low view of sin, an anti-supernatural bias, and an ongoing questioning of the place of authority and tradition.[18]

Some theologians attempted to merge or synthesize the Christian tradition with ideas coming forth from the Enlightenment movement. While many joined in this effort, chief among these was Friedrich Schleiermacher (1768–1834). With his book *On Religion, Speeches To Its Cultured Despisers* (1799), Schleiermacher called for a way in which the Christian faith could be heard afresh in a rapidly changing culture, attempting to adapt the Christian faith to this new mode of thinking. Such efforts to translate the Christian faith to the changing times were not just attempts to make the Christian faith relevant or to bring Christianity to a place where it could be heard afresh. This new movement, known as liberalism, transformed the Christian faith into something quite different. The result was a lost connection with the great history of the Christian movement, a disconnect with the great tradition.

Much of the work by Christian thinkers in the various fields of thought over the past three centuries has been attempts to wrestle with the implications of Enlightenment and post-Enlightenment thought. Many have in various and significant ways sought to reclaim the best of the Christian intellectual tradition for the modern world: Congregationalists such as Jonathan Edwards (1703–1758); Reformed thinkers such as Abraham Kuyper (1837–1920) and B. B. Warfield (1851–1921); neo-Reformed theologians such as Karl Barth (1886–1968); Baptists such as A. H. Strong (1836–1921) and Carl F. H. Henry (1913–2003); Lutherans such as J. A. O. Preus II (1920–1994); British Catholic and Anglican scholars such as Cardinal Newman (1801–1890), G. K. Chesterton (1874–1936), and C. S. Lewis (1898–1963); Methodists such as John Wesley

---

[18]See the various discussions in Alister McGrath, *Heresy* (San Francisco: HarperOne, 2009), 175–222; Harold O. J. Brown, *Heresies* (Garden City, NY: Doubleday, 1984); Jonathan Wright, *Heretics* (Boston: Houghton Mifflin Harcourt, 2011); Ben Walsh and Michael Ward, *Heresies and How to Avoid Them* (London: SPCK, 2007); David S. Dockery, ed., *The Challenge of Postmodernism* (Grand Rapids, MI: Baker, 1995, 2001); and G. R. Evans, *A Brief History of Heresy* (London: Blackwell, 2003).

(1703–1791) and Thomas Oden (1931–); and influencers of contemporary global Christianity such as Francis Cardinal Arinze and Luke Orambi in Africa, together with Siga Aries and Wallace Louie in Asia.

CONCLUSION: THE CHRISTIAN INTELLECTUAL TRADITION FOR THE TWENTY-FIRST CENTURY

We now find ourselves in the global context of the twenty-first century, a context that presents not only great challenges but also amazing and new opportunities.[19] The "new" atheism, the expansion of secularism, and the rise of religious pluralism in the Western world often cause Christians to become discouraged. Yet new opportunities are arising to reclaim the best of the Christian intellectual tradition, not only in theology but also in literature, the arts, the sciences, and all areas of life. This Crossway series is dedicated to such an effort. In doing so, we are encouraged by the Christian movement in Asia, Africa, and Latin America.[20] God's Spirit is moving around the globe, and it is time for us to see with new eyes and fresh perspectives. What is needed is a shared effort to reclaim and advance the heart of the Christian intellectual tradition, shaped by a renewed commitment to Trinitarian orthodoxy, to a faithful transgenerational, transcontinental, and multiethnic movement that stands or falls on primary Christian beliefs.

In order to recover the Christian intellectual tradition for our contemporary context, we are calling not only for a renewed emphasis on faith and reason, along with serious interpretation of Scripture, but also for shared commitments to the divine nature and authority of God's written Word, to the deity and humanity

---

[19]Among many sources to which we could point, one that seems helpful in summarizing well these effects is Thomas Oden, *Requiem: A Lament in Three Movements* (Nashville: Abingdon, 1995). Also see Charles Taylor, *A Secular Age* (Cambridge, MA: Belknap, 2007); R. Albert Mohler Jr., *Atheism Remix: A Christian Confronts the New Atheism* (Wheaton, IL: Crossway, 2008).

[20]See Roland Spliesgant, et al., *A History of Christianity in Asia, Africa, and Latin America* (Grand Rapids, MI: Eerdmans, 2007); Thomas Oden, *How Africa Shaped the Christian Mind* (Downers Grove, IL: InterVarsity, 2010).

of Jesus Christ, to a heartfelt confession regarding the holy Trinity, to the uniqueness of the gospel message and the enabling work of God's Holy Spirit, to salvation by grace through faith, to the church universal, to the hope of the coming kingdom, and to the sacredness of life and family. A model of dynamic orthodoxy must be recovered in conversation with Nicaea, Chalcedon, Augustine, Bernard, Luther, Calvin, Wesley, the Pietists, and the influential global Christian leaders of the twenty-first century in order to reclaim and build upon the great Christian intellectual tradition.

The great tradition of Christian thinking not only shaped biblical and theological understanding but also provided a vast resource for philosophy, art, music, literature, drama, architecture, law, political and social thought, and other forms of cultural and academic engagement. Interestingly, Christian reflection and devotional practices were influenced by the work of this significant heritage. The next three chapters in this book offer more specific ways that the Christian intellectual tradition, a tradition grounded and rooted in the *consensus fidei* of the Christian church through the centuries, can be reclaimed and advanced for our day.[21]

---

[21]For an insightful look at what is being called for in this volume, see Jonathan Hill, *What Has Christianity Ever Done for Us? How It Shaped the Modern World* (Downers Grove, IL: InterVarsity, 2005); and J. I. Packer and Thomas C. Oden, *One Faith: The Evangelical Consensus* (Downers Grove, IL InterVarsity, 2004).

3

THE SHAPING OF THE GREAT TRADITION

It is difficult to be a Christian by oneself. . . . Christ ordained that the
Christian is to be nourished and supported by other Christians . . .
the solidarity with the Christian church through the ages, with its store of
wisdom and with its great intellectual tradition. . . . Christian students and
thinkers need to take advantage of the spiritual and intellectual interplay
that can be found in what the creeds refer to as "the communion of saints."
Gene Edward Veith, *Love God with All Your Mind* (1987)

The "integration of faith and reason" makes for a nice mantra.
You can find it in attractive brochures from innumerable Christian
universities, assuring prospective students—or, at least, their par-
ents—that each of these schools has some vague connection to a
religious tradition, that some kind of chapel program is still maintained, and that faculty members have some basic connection to
church and Christian piety.

Unfortunately, as we saw in our introductory examples in
chapter 1, that's about all it means in many contexts because
of the dichotomy that has arisen between faith and knowledge.
Another reason that the "integration of faith and reason" has
perhaps become little more than a rhetorical gesture in some
Christian contexts may be that the Bible itself has become margin-
alized within our academic discourse. This might seem an unlikely
conclusion. In popular perceptions, Christians in general and
evangelicals in particular are quintessentially biblicistic. Wheaton
College's statement of faith, for example, reads: "We believe that

God has revealed Himself and His truth in the created order, in the Scriptures, and supremely in Jesus Christ, and that the Scriptures of the Old and New Testaments are verbally inspired by God and inerrant in the original writing, so that they are fully trustworthy and of supreme and final authority in all they say."

As it happens, both of us are Southern Baptists, and we Baptists can extol the Scriptures with the best of them. The Bible, we like to say, is inspired, infallible, inerrant; we love those *i* words, and we can add a few more if you like: immeasurable, inimitable, invincible, and irrefragable. And yet, for all this, the Bible remains, in much of the Christian world, an inert (a bad *i* word) artifact from antiquity. Too often we construe its authority as a kind of divine reference book, a sort of inspired manual, that can be understood quite apart from the Christian heritage of biblical interpretation, theology, and wisdom across the centuries, something quite contrary to the pattern set forth in our opening chapters.[1]

THE PATTERN OF CHRISTIAN TRUTH

If we are to talk meaningfully about the integration of faith and reason—the joining of Scripture and the disciplines at which a Christian university ought to aim—then our next step beyond understanding the primacy of biblical interpretation calls for revisiting the development of Christian doctrine. We need to discern "the pattern of Christian truth," to borrow a phrase that H. E. W. Turner used as the title of an important book he published as a result of his famous Bampton Lectures at Oxford University in 1954.[2]

Turner was responding to *Orthodoxy and Heresy in Earliest Christianity*, a book by the German scholar Walter Bauer, originally published in German in 1934. Bauer contended that what

---

[1]Portions of this chapter have been adapted from Timothy George, "The Pattern of Christian Truth," *First Things* 154 (2005): 21–25; David S. Dockery, *Renewing Minds* (Nashville: Broadman, 2007–2008), 59–66.
[2]See H. E. W. Turner, *The Pattern of Christian Truth* (London: Mobray, 1954).

emerged as mainstream Christian orthodoxy in the second and third centuries was merely one strand of a very diffuse Christian movement and no more normative for the life of faith than the other trajectories we can identify in apostolic and post-apostolic times. Bauer's thesis has, of course, become the reigning orthodoxy within the wider academy. Witness Elaine Pagel's books on Gnosticism and the *Gospel of Thomas*—to say nothing of Dan Brown's blockbuster novel *The Da Vinci Code*.

In response, Turner claimed there was a discernible *pattern* of Christian truth, a pattern derived from the apostolic witness and maintained across time as the *depositum fidei* or what the New Testament calls "the faith that was once for all delivered to the saints" (Jude 3). This pattern is embedded, like a genetic code, in the inspired text of Scripture itself. But only by having to confront counter-narratives—by having to respond to heresy—does the community of faith recognize this pattern with clarity and set forth creeds and confessions of faith to guard the integrity of its worship and proclamation.

The word *heresy* dredges up the flames of Smithfield, the tortures of the Inquisition, and the *malleus maleficarum* ("the hammer of the witches"). Indeed, heresy hunting and witch burning seem almost synonymous today. Yet the first generation of Christians—as the story is told in Galatians 1:9 and 1 John 4:1–3—found themselves confronted with an alternative pattern of teaching that they could not allow if they were to remain faithful to their Lord. This was not a conflict over secondary matters about which sincere Christians might differ—say, whether the third trumpet sounds before the forth seal is broken in the book of Revelation. No, heresy is a deliberate perversion, a "choice" (*hairesis* in Greek), to break with the primary pattern of Christian truth and to promulgate a doctrine that undermines the gospel and destroys the unity of the Christian church. A church that cannot distinguish heresy from truth, or, even worse, a church that no longer thinks this is worth doing, is a church that has lost its right to bear witness to the transforming gospel of Jesus Christ, who declared himself to be not only the way and the life but also the truth.

But there is a positive side to heresy as well—in the sense that the history of heresy is the shadow side of the development of doctrine. In the light of its corruption, we can see, retrospectively, the splendor and beauty of the divine revelation embedded in Holy Scripture. In its confrontation with heresiarchs, the church, as we saw in chapter 1, learned to read the Scriptures in a way that should still inform us today.[3]

RESPONSE TO MARCION (CA. 85–160)

Marcion was included in our discussion in chapter 1; we now take a more detailed look. A shipbuilder born in Pontus, near the Black Sea, Marcion grew up in the church, the son of a bishop. Having amassed great wealth, he migrated around AD 139 to Rome, where he made a large donation to the church. For five years he wrote and taught in Rome, gathering a following so large that, when he was excommunicated in 144, he is said to have carried half the church with him.

According to Irenaeus, Marcion once encountered Polycarp of Smyrna on the streets of Rome and asked, "Do you know who I am?"—to which Polycarp replied, "I know the first-born of Satan." Marcion's aim was to pull Christianity out from its Jewish soil, and to do this he had to divide creation from redemption. The God of the Old Testament, Marcion said, is not the Father of Jesus (whom Marcion called instead "the Alien God"). The Jewish God was rather a kind of demiurge, like the one in Plato's *Timaeus*: a sort of divine craftsman who reshaped the primordial, chaotic matter of the universe.

Make no mistake: Marcion thought his demiurge a real god.

---

[3]See Alister McGrath, *Heresy* (San Francisco: Harper One, 2009); Harold O. J. Brown, *Heresies* (Garden City, NY: Doubleday, 1984); Ben Walsh and Michael Ward, *Heresies and How to Avoid Them* (London: SPCK, 2007).

It was that god who had made a covenant with the Jews and gave them their law. He had promised one day to send them a messiah, and he would keep the promise. But Jesus, Marcion says, is not that messiah. Jesus is instead the emissary of the Alien Father. Jesus came to offer an alternative way of salvation, one that bypassed the world of matter, the world of bugs and mosquitoes and crocodiles and vipers, the world of birth and begetting, of sexuality and marriage. Jesus did not experience a natural, human birth: "Away," Marcion said, "with that poor inn, those mean swaddling clothes, and that rough stable." The true Christ could not have assumed a material body that participated in the created world, for such a body would have been "stuffed with excrement." Significantly, Marcion would admit married persons to baptism in his church only if they took a vow to abstain from all sexual intercourse. Sex was anathema because of—not in spite of—procreation, since the material body was a curse and an indignity.

Marcion shared his Docetism and anti-materialism with the Gnostics of his day, but he had a different, more radical, way of justifying his beliefs. Early on, many Christian interpreters resorted to nonliteral and allegorical readings of the Old Testament, especially of such difficult passages as the imprecatory psalms. Marcion, however, urged the rejection of the entire Old Testament. God's dealings with humankind through Christ stood in no relation to any previous dispensation but were radically new and radically other. Having rejected the Old Testament as legitimate Scripture for Christians, Marcion concocted his own alternative, a two-part document consisting of his "Evangelium" and "Apostolicum." The Evangelium was an expurgated version of Luke that omitted the messy birth narratives, while the Apostolicum was a carefully edited version of ten of Paul's epistles. (Unlike his Gnostic contemporaries, Marcion claimed no private tradition of secret sayings or oral transmissions.)

In responding to Marcion, the church reaffirmed two principles of primary importance in the pattern of Christian truth. Indeed all subsequent theology is to some degree a working out of these two principles: the coinherence of creation and redemption and the fundamental continuity of the Old and New Testaments.[4]

While the process of canon formation required several centuries of controversy, debate, and assessment—as the church sorted through not only the challenge of Marcion, who wanted to truncate the canon, but also others, such as the Montanists, who tried to expand it—the fundamental direction of this process was set in the context of the earlier debate. Insofar as we orthodox Christians today accept the Scriptures as a discrete corpus of inspired writings, we do so because we stand on this side of the great divide of the second century's battle for the Bible.

ARIUS (CA. 250-336)

If Marcion taught the church one lesson about what Christianity was *not*, Arius taught us another in the fourth century. One question—How is Jesus of Nazareth related to the God who created all things other than himself by his almighty, sovereign power?—was at the heart of the struggle between Arius, a presbyter in the church of Alexandria, and his bishop Athanasius.

Arius had a serious theological point: God's innermost being or essence, he said, cannot be shared, or communicated, with anyone else. "We know," he declared, "there is one God, alone unbegotten, alone eternal, alone without beginning, alone true, alone immortal." God is thus utterly transcendent, self-sufficient, and all-powerful. What's more, this God guards his divinity jealously—a parsimonious God, a God so self-contained in isolation and absoluteness that the very thought of sharing his "essence" with anyone, even with a "Son," was abhorrent to him.

Against this view, Athanasius and the orthodox Fathers who gathered at the Council of Nicaea in 325 declared their belief "in

---

[4]See Gregg R. Allison, *Historical Theology* (Grand Rapids, MI: Zondervan, 2011), 39–42.

one Lord Jesus Christ, the only begotten son of God, begotten of his Father before all worlds, God of God, Light of Light, very God of very God, begotten, not made, being of one substance with the Father." If Jesus was not one substance with the Father, the council said, then he was neither worthy to be worshiped nor capable of redeeming the world.

Arius had ridiculed the idea that God could "beget a son," as unitarianism of every kind has always done. But Athanasius, and the theologians in the Nicene tradition who followed him, sought to explain the "begottenness" of the Son in a way that avoided both the sterility of Arius's God and the crass literalism derived from Greek mythology. The Nicene formula described the Son as being both the *same* in substance with the Father and also in some way *distinct from* the Father: he was God *from* God, Light *from* Light, very God *from* very God.

The challenge was to explain this "from-ness" without violating the sameness. This they did by declaring that the Son was begotten—but not in the way human fathers beget or generate their earthly children. The Son of the heavenly Father was begotten from all eternity. He did not "come to be" at a point in time, but from eternity the Father and the Son have existed in a relation of total and mutual self-giving. Thus, far from compromising God's fundamental reality, communicability and relationship are constitutive of it. This is what the Bible means when it declares that "God is love" (1 John 4:8, 16).

It is often said that the doctrine of the Trinity was the result of Christian capitulation to Greek philosophy. In fact, it was the exact opposite. Arius was the one who pushed the implications of philosophical monism and consequently had to portray Christ in mythological terms as neither God nor human but rather as a sort of demi-god who, though the most exalted of all creatures, was still only a creature.[5]

---

[5] See Alister McGrath, *Historical Theology* (Oxford: Blackwell, 1998), 33–51.

The doctrine of the Trinity belongs to the pattern of Christian truth because without it we cannot really understand the narrative of Jesus as the story of God, and if the story of Jesus is ultimately anything other than the story of God, there is no gospel. The doctrine of the Trinity is necessary for understanding the Bible's overarching account of what God has said and done in history. Such a framework makes the Scriptures not just a disparate collection of interesting documents from the world of antiquity, but one single unitary *Bible*. It allows us to use the word *Scripture* as a singular, collective noun. This is a lesson Arius has helped us to learn.

PELAGIUS (CA. 354–420)

Both Marcion and Arius were from the East. For a final example of the usefulness of heretics in forcing us to understand the pattern of Christian truth, we turn to a Western heretic: Pelagius. Born around 354 in the British Isles, at the very edge of what was then the civilized world, Pelagius had piercing eyes and red hair and carried the family name of Morgan, facts which have led some to think he may have come from Ireland. In any event, he had the scent of Celtic asceticism about him, and when he moved to Rome he was deeply offended by the laxity he saw among Christians there.

He was especially infuriated when he overheard Augustine's prayer *Domine, da quod iubes et iube quod vis*: "O Lord, give what You command, and command whatever You will." This kind of devotion, Pelagius thought, undercut the moral nerve of Christian faith. If we are not able to obey God's commandments by ourselves, then why had he given them in the first place? Salvation must come from the performance of good works and the fulfillment of obligations laid down by God.

Pelagian theology begins with the notion that Adam was created mortal: he would have died even if he had never sinned. Thus, we do not inherit death from Adam as the punishment for sin. Nor do we inherit the sin itself. According to Pelagius, sin is transmitted by imitation, not propagation. Human beings are born without sin, and they commit sins only by following the bad examples of others.

This means that grace is not opposed to nature but rather is present within nature itself. With the law in the Old Testament and Christ in the New, God has given us the perfect rule book and the perfect rule keeper, but nothing more—for salvation, like sin, is by imitation. This means that perfection in this life is possible. Pelagius did not say that it was easy. He did not claim to be perfect himself. But he did believe that, in addition to Jesus, there were perfect people who always obeyed all of God's commands. It is the worst kind of defeatism, he thought, to tell Christians in advance that perfection was unattainable. Indeed, for Pelagius, predestination is subordinate to foreknowledge: when the Bible speaks of God's predestination of the elect, it is merely speaking of his ability to see into the future and ratify in advance what he knows human beings will do by their own efforts.

In the course of the Pelagian controversy, Augustine answered that Pelagius had turned the whole of Christian theology upside down. Death is not natural but radically inimical to human life, an "enemy" to be overcome, as Paul put it. The moment Adam sinned, he began "verging toward old age and death." Developing a robust doctrine of original sin, which emphasized the seminal and corporate identity of the human family, Augustine argued that the human situation is far more serious than Pelagius allowed. Only a supernatural work of God, which comes to sinners from beyond themselves, can make any real difference in our standing before a holy God. Christians can indeed make great progress in their walk with God, and they should be encouraged to do so, but sin is an ever-present reality with which we must struggle until we draw our last breath. Thus every day we need to offer again this petition from the Lord's Prayer: "Forgive us our debts" (Matt. 6:12).

Following Paul, Augustine grounded his understanding of

predestination in God's *eudokia*, his "good pleasure," as the King James Version translates that term in Ephesians 1:5. It is important to note that Augustine affirms the intactness of human free will even after the fall: it is still we who act and love and choose, and we who are therefore responsible morally for what we do. But the will has become so thoroughly susceptible to pride and self-seeking that it is disposed now to choose objects of desire that lead it further and further away from God. In other words, human free will has been so weakened by sin and the fall that it has become, as Luther would say, *incurvatus in se*—"curved in on itself," like a coil or a spring. We are *liberi, sed non liberati*—"free, but not freed." Augustine knew that we were created by God for fellowship with him, and that our hearts would always be restless until they found true rest in him. But this kind of reorientation required *gratia operans*, "the operation of divine grace." As Jesus says in John 15:5 (one of Augustine's favorite Bible verses): "Apart from me you can do nothing."

Even though Pelagius was condemned as a heretic at the Council of Ephesus in 431, one year after Augustine's death, his ideas continue to influence the way we understand the human situation, not only in the optimistic anthropology of liberal Protestantism and the lingering semi-Pelagianism of some Roman Catholics, but also in a sort of "can-do" fashion, all too prominent in many sectors of American Christianity, which give prominence to positive thinking and self-improvement. Benjamin B. Warfield may have been right when he said that the Reformation was the triumph of Augustine's theology of grace over his doctrine of the church, but in a broader sense *sola gratia* is the common heritage of both historic Protestantism and faithful Catholicism, just as it is the shared confession of both classical Calvinism and the Arminianism of John Wesley.[6] These are lessons Pelagius has helped us to learn.

---

[6] See Jonathan Hill, *The History of Christian Thought* (Downers Grove, IL: InterVarsity, 2003), 78–91.

IMPLICATIONS FOR CHRISTIAN LEARNING AND TEACHING

If the response to these three heretics constitutes part of the permanent, irreducible, and irreversible pattern of Christian truth, then this has important implications for Christian scholars in all disciplines. We are not free to throw in a Gnostic gospel or two—or to delete embarrassing miracles or "doubtful" Jesus sayings—and regard our new configuration as having the same valence as the canonical books of the Old and New Testaments. Nor can we present Jesus of Nazareth as merely one savior among many or the way of salvation as a form of self-enhancement.

As Christians who accept the church's *regula fidei* ("rule of faith") and who stand Sunday after Sunday to recite the Apostles' Creed and the Nicene Creed, we are not free to view the Bible as though we had it at our disposal, as though we ourselves were not claimed by its story, as though we had already mastered this ancient document and could now move on to other bodies of knowledge without the discernment we have learned from Scripture. When Calvin began his *Institutes* with the sentence, "Nearly all the wisdom we possess consists of two parts: the knowledge of God and of ourselves," he didn't mean that we should first earn a PhD in systematic theology, and then, with the knowledge of God safely under our belt, switch disciplines and go on to earn a second PhD in, say, psychology. The *duplex cognitio* Calvin refers to is not sequential but correlative: we cannot know ourselves without knowing that we are at once finite and fallen creatures of God. Nor can we know God without knowing ourselves as persons made in his image, as objects of his judgment and love.

This is not to say, of course, that we cannot learn a great deal about the world of nature and history and science and politics and art quite apart from the story of God and his creatures as it is told in the Bible and confessed in the creeds of the Christian faith. Of course, we can and we must. But as believing scholars committed to the pattern of Christian truth, we must never forget that the usefulness of such abstract knowledge is limited. By itself, abstraction will always lead us away from what is truly real. Divorced from the biblical narrative, a purely abstract knowledge becomes not only self-referential but also self-defeating, fatuous, and sterile. It, too, will curve back in on itself.

As the noted theologian Robert Jenson once put it: "Scripture's story is not part of some larger narrative; it is itself the larger narrative of which all other true narratives are parts. And so do not when reading Scripture try to figure out how what you are reading fits into some larger story; for there *is* no larger story."[7] This is true whether we are talking about biology, political science, or aesthetics. Disconnected from the biblical story, such disciplines can tell us how things work but not what they are for; how to clone a human baby but not whether this should be done; how to construct an atomic bomb but not whether it should be used; how to build a maximum security prison but not how to treat the prisoners. Without some teleology, there is no flourishing and no future for the human community.

This way of reading the Bible has important implications for the various disciplines. Against Marcion the church decided to retain the Old Testament as Christian Scripture and rejected his division of creation and redemption. In doing so, it validated what we might call the "principle of luminous particularity," the principle that no object in nature, and no event in history, is an isolated, opaque fact closed in on itself. Each is, rather, a translucent window onto a whole pattern of human experience. This means that we must approach the world with a profound respect for the numinous character that it possesses—not because it is some kind of earth goddess but by virtue of its having been created by the triune God.

In its struggle with Arius, the church affirmed the central

---

[7]Robert W. Jenson, "Scripture's Authority in the Church," in *The Art of Reading Scripture*, ed. Ellen F. Davis and Richard B. Hays (Grand Rapids, MI: Eerdmans, 2003), 34. See also Jenson's essay, "What If It Were True?," in *Reflections: Center of Theological Inquiry* 4 (2001): 2–21.

axiom of the Christian faith, summarized by John in the prologue to his Gospel: "And the Word became flesh and dwelt among us" (John 1:14). The church has always had to insist on the reality of the incarnation against Docetists, Neoplatonists, and deists of all kinds, against the kind of God Thomas Hardy described as "a dreaming, dark, dumb Thing that turns the handle of this idle show." This hideous caricature is widely accepted in today's world and is at the root of much contemporary atheism. Against all of this the church echoes the language of Scripture and declares, in the words of Ignatius of Antioch, that Jesus Christ was *truly* born, *truly* lived, *truly* died, and *truly* rose—*altheōs, altheōs, altheōs*, the Greek adverb resounding like a gong through the debates of the early church.

Finally, from the struggle with Pelagius, we learn the practice of humility before the mystery of the holy. Augustine discerned in Pelagius the same scorning of humility that he had witnessed among the Neoplatonists. This is an occupational hazard for all of us who stand with one foot in *ecclesia* (the church), and the other in *schola* (the academy). We may be Augustinians in our theology, but we are all socialized to be Pelagians in our profession, to exaggerate the importance of personal effort and personal worthiness. We drill this into our children and students from kindergarten on. As administrators who recommend colleagues for promotion and tenure in our institutions, and as trustees who vote on such recommendations and other contexts, we know all too well the institutional constraints that reinforce this kind of academic Pelagianism from which none of us is exempt.

Augustine made a distinction between a way of knowing he called "scientia"—the image of a man hanging off a cliff by his fingernails, frenetically digging and scratching, straining every nerve until his fingernails are embedded with the dirt and blood of his exertion. He said there is another way of knowing, "sapientia": wisdom. And this often comes to us as an unexpected insight. In such moments cognition becomes recognition, and you know that this is not achievement but gift. This is the kind of knowledge that generates humility before the mystery of the holy.

Augustine has not always been very well received in the East, but we think he would like this statement from Theaphon the Recluse, a Russian Orthodox bishop of the nineteenth century: "The principal thing is to stand before God with intellect in the heart, and to go on standing before Him unceasingly day and night, until the end of life." In such a summons to humility we find the implicit covenant of all our dialogues and our vocation as followers of the Lamb and students in the school of Christ. Our next building block will lead us to a further exploration of the importance of a confessional faith in shaping and advancing the Christian intellectual tradition.

4

THE THEOLOGICAL COMMITMENTS OF THE GREAT TRADITION

Christianity is more than a set of devotional practices. . . . It is also
a way of thinking about God, about human beings, about the world,
and history. For Christians, thinking is part of believing.

Robert Louis Wilken, *The Spirit of Early Christian Thought* (2003)

Jaroslav Pelikan famously defined Christian doctrine as what the
church of Jesus Christ believes, teaches, and confesses on the basis
of the Word of God.[1] What can we make of such a definition
in the postmodern, secularizing academy? Even many so-called
church-related colleges and universities, including those that are
not embarrassed to admit some putative connection to a religious
tradition, are hesitant to be too definite about their Christian
identity. No self-respecting, accredited academic institution wants
to be known as a center of indoctrination, a word that connotes
high-handed, authoritarian, brow-beating pedagogy, though the
basic definition of indoctrinate is simply "to instruct in doctrines,
principles, theories, and beliefs."

If "indoctrination" conjures up too many ghosts from the
fundamentalist outback, how about "formation"? That's a more
acceptable word, and a better one perhaps, because it implies a
more holistic approach to Christian nurture. Formation involves

---

[1]See Jaroslav Pelikan, *The Christian Tradition*, 5 vols. (Chicago: University of Chicago Press, 1971–89).

more than the transfer of cognitive data from one mind to another. It involves development, growth, community, and service to others. But genuine formation—spiritual, intellectual, theological, liturgical, aesthetic—will take place in a school of Christian higher education only where there is both the requirement and the freedom "to instruct in doctrines, principles, theories, and beliefs." This chapter will examine some of the principal elements of the confessional heritage that has been and remains indispensible for the intellectual and spiritual formation of followers of Jesus Christ, whether such formation is done in families, monasteries, churches, schools, or universities.[2]

THE FAITH ONCE FOR ALL ENTRUSTED TO THE SAINTS

Let's begin by examining the word *faith* itself. In the letter of Jude we find this statement: "Beloved, although I was very eager to write to you about our common salvation, I found it necessary to write appealing to you to contend for the faith that was once for all delivered to the saints" (v. 3). Faith is used in the New Testament in two senses, which in the history of theology have been designated by two Latin expressions: *fides quae*, "the faith *that* we believe," and *fides qua*, "the faith *by which* we believe." In Jude, reference is made to *the* faith that was once for all entrusted to the saints.

Jude is an important book because it was written at a time of great crisis in the life of the early church—a crisis that came both from without and from within. Christians were really beginning to feel the effects of harassment and persecution, as we read in the book of Acts in some of the early accounts of Christians facing hostility from the governing authorities. But when Jude was written—we do not know exactly when that was, perhaps toward the

[2]Portions of this chapter have been adapted from Timothy George, "The Faith, My Faith, the Church's Faith," in *Southern Baptists, Evangelicals, and the Future of Denominationalism*, ed. David S. Dockery (Nashville: Broadman, 2011), 81–93; and David S. Dockery, *Renewing Minds* (Nashville: Broadman, 2007–2008), 124–37.

end of the first century—Christians were facing more sustained hostility, open violence, and persecution from the environing culture, from the Roman Empire. Perhaps Jude was written following the persecutions unleashed by that sadistic pyromaniac, Emperor Nero. When you visit Rome today, you see the Coliseum. The Coliseum was originally a swimming pool for Nero's great palace on the hill above. In one of his banquets, Nero had Christians in Rome rounded up and tied to poles and set on fire so that as people came to dine, they passed these burning Christians—living lampposts—on the way to the banquet. In those days, human life was cheap and none more so than that of Christians and slaves. Jude was written in that kind of environment, when discipleship was costly, and the cross more than a metaphor.

In that environment, Jude wrote to these believers and said: "I wanted to write to you about something else. I wanted to write to you about our common salvation. I wanted to write to you about the wonderful, glorious fact that we have been delivered from darkness and placed into light through the grace of our Lord Jesus Christ." What could be more important, more wonderful, more glorious than that—our salvation in Christ? But Jude says that there was indeed something more important. There was something more urgent and more pressing, something that he just had to write about. Jude just had twenty-four verses in his short epistle, and he could not say everything, so he had to prioritize the message that God gave him to deliver. He boiled it down to what was urgent: I *had* to write to you.

What is this thing that motivates Jude? I *had* to write and urge you to contend for *fides quae*, the faith *that* we confess. Now what is *the* faith? Well, *the* faith is the essential content of the Christian *kerygma*, the Christian message—the proclamation of Jesus Christ as Lord of lords and King of kings; the way, the truth, and the life. *The* faith is what it is we have to say and tell the world about what God has once and for all done in Jesus Christ. This phrase is used a number of times in the New Testament, not only here in Jude 3, but also in 2 Timothy 4:7, where Paul says, "I have fought the good fight, I have finished the race, I have kept *the* faith." Or in Ephesians 4:5, where we are admonished to hold forth one Lord, one faith, and one baptism. Again, in 1 Corinthians 16:13, Paul writes to the saints at Corinth and encourages them to stand firm in *the* faith. Now, *the* faith as it is used here in the singular and particular sense is what came to be summarized and passed on to successive generations of Christians as the Apostles' Creed, the rule of faith, and later the Nicene Creed of the early church.[3]

Why do we need creeds or confessional statements in the first place? We know it is popular in some circles to talk about "no creed but the Bible." But sometimes that phrase, "no creed but the Bible," is just a shibboleth for neither creed nor the Bible. There is a sense in which "no creed but the Bible" is a good phrase if we mean "no creedalism, only the Bible," because we do not want to elevate any humanly constructed statement, however venerable or wonderful it may be, to a level equal with or much less above the written Word of God in Holy Scripture. Nor do we hold any humanly constructed statement of faith to be beyond reform, beyond revision, beyond restatement. We always must subject our statements of faith and the creeds of the church to the written Word of God. The Bible is the *norma normans*, the norming norm, to which all our beliefs and our practices must be held accountable. Nor do we want the state, the government, the civil authority, to be writing creeds and imposing them on God's people. This is a violation of religious liberty. So, in those three senses—no creed that is above the Bible, no creed that is irrevisable, and no creed that is imposed by civil authority—it is right to protest against the abuse of creeds. But Jude has something else in mind.

That word "entrusted," or, as the KJV and ESV translate,

---

[3]See Christopher R. Seitz, *Nicene Christianity* (Grand Rapids, MI: Brazos, 2001); also Frances M. Young, *From Nicaea to Chalcedon*, 2nd ed. (Grand Rapids, MI: Baker, 2010).

"delivered," to the saints is itself a very interesting word. It is the word for handing on, handing down, from one generation to another. Or you may think of it in terms of a race. We have a relay, and one person gives the baton to another runner, and he carries it toward the finish line. That is the idea, and this word *traditor* in Latin is very close to another word, one that sounds similar in English, *traitor*. There is a fine line between being one who *hands on* the faith intact, a *traditor*, and one who *betrays* the faith, a traitor. They are very close words etymologically and semantically. Those who have been charged with preaching and teaching the Word of God must be careful that in our efforts to pass on the faith, we do not betray it.

In the early centuries when the Roman authorities came to a Christian town or village, their first demand was, "Give us the books." They did not care so much about the church buildings and the rest of the things the Christians had. But the books—by which they meant, of course, the Bible, the Word of God, the Holy Scriptures—were important. Their theory was that if they could destroy the Bible, they could destroy the faith. If they could burn the books, they could obliterate the Christian message. They were on to something.

Why do we need creeds? We have the Bible, after all. Why do we need these humanly constructed statements of faith, the creeds and confessions of the church, to proclaim *the* faith, once for all entrusted, passed on?

Our confessions of faith are like guardrails. When you are traveling dangerous roads, you are glad someone has put those guardrails in place. Now you do not want to confuse the guardrails with the road and start driving up there on the guardrails— then danger is really imminent! Stay on the road. The road is Jesus Christ. He said: "I am the way [the road], and the truth, and the life" (John 14:6). But we need guardrails as we are tempted this way and that in the history of the church, guardrails to keep us on the road guided by the light that is the Holy Scriptures: "Your word is a lamp to my feet and a light to my path" (Ps. 119:105).

Just as there are two expressions, *fides quae* and *fides qua*—the faith *that* we believe and the faith *by which* we believe—so too there are two words in Latin for faith, and they figured prominently in the debates of the Reformation. One word is *assensus*. You can tell what it means just by the way that it sounds in English. *Assensus*—to assent to, to agree with, to say yes to. It is a part of the faith *that* we confess. Let us not downgrade this kind of faith. It is a part of the objective content and deposit of faith that is true for everybody everywhere. This is what *the* faith means. Does a tree that falls in the forest make a sound whether you are there to hear it or not? Did Pluto revolve around the sun before it was "discovered" over eighty years ago?

There is an objective content, a deposit of faith given by God as a part of the divine revelation of himself in Jesus Christ and in the Holy Scriptures. That is *assensus*. Say yes to that. Assent to this content is absolutely necessary, but it is not sufficient. There is another word, *fiducia*, and we have a word in English, *fiduciary*, related to that as well. *Fiduciary* is a word that has to do with holding something in trust for someone else. It involves a personal commitment you make yourself, and this is a word that Martin Luther used to describe saving, believing faith; personal trust; letting loose of yourself. In German, it is *Gelassenheit*. We do not have a good English equivalent for the beautiful German word, *gelassen,* to let loose of yourself, let go of yourself, stop depending on yourself, and throw yourself wildly into the arms of Jesus Christ. That is saving faith. That is *fiducial* faith. That is when *the* faith becomes *my* faith.

In the early years of the Reformation, Thomas Bilney came to Cambridge, England. He was a scholar and was interested in studying the classics, the great texts of antiquity. It was just at the time when Desiderius Erasmus translated the Bible into Latin based on the critical edition of the New Testament in Greek that he had published at Basel in 1516. When Bilney came to Cambridge, Erasmus had been there just a few years before, working on his Latin translation. Bilney was particularly interested in reading it because it was not in the old medieval Vulgate Latin but was all spruced up in Ciceronian Latin, and he loved that, the challenge of it, the excitement of it. But as he began to read this Bible just for the sheer literary joy and pleasure of taking in the beauty of the Latin language, he came across a verse, 1 Timothy 1:15, in which Paul says, "I give unto you that which is a true and faithful statement" (AT). Well, the old Latin translation would have been *fidelis sermo*, a faithful word, a true word, but in the new Erasmian translation, that word "faithful" was rendered *certa*, believable, credible, assured. When Bilney read that word and the text that followed, where Paul says, "Christ Jesus came into the world to save sinners," it struck him in his heart that the verse was meant for him. He was a sinner and Christ Jesus had come into the world to save him, even him. He says that when reading that verse, "Immediately I felt a marvelous comfort and quietness, insomuch that my bruised bones leapt for joy." That is when *the* faith became *his* faith.

David Bebbington, an eminent Scottish historian of evangelicalism, has talked about the great traits, the characteristics of evangelicalism: the Bible—we believe the Bible is the Word of God. We are committed to the understanding of Jesus and his atoning work on the cross. In addition, we believe in the mission of the church—he uses the word *activism*—we go into the world in Jesus's name to share his good news to everybody everywhere. All of this is related, Bebbington says, to another characteristic, the new birth, which is to be converted, turned around, changed—to use a little more theological language, regenerated—by the power of the Holy Spirit.[4] As long as *the* faith remains detached, divorced, distant, as long as *the* faith is simply a system of doctrine codified

---

[4] See David Bebbington, *The Dominance of Evangelicalism* (Downers Grove, IL: InterVarsity, 2005).

in a systematic theology, as long as *the* faith is kept at arm's length, then we are like Nicodemus who came to Jesus by night and said to him, "Rabbi, we know that you are a teacher come from God, for no one can do these signs that you do unless God is with him" (John 3:2). Jesus said to him, "Nicodemus, you must be born again—born from above, born anew." That is the message that faithful Christ followers have proclaimed to the world. We proclaim this message in all its fullness to those who need to know that Jesus Christ has come into the world. Just like Thomas Bilney. He became a believer because he read that one verse of Scripture, and his life was changed. It cost him something, for in 1531 he was burned alive at the stake in the city of Norwich. He became one of the first martyrs of the English Reformation.

THE CHURCH'S FAITH

We have discussed *the* faith and *my* faith. We want now to focus on the *church's* faith. In the history of theology, *the* faith and *my* faith taken in isolation from one another have led to some dead ends that we must avoid at all costs. *The* faith without *my* faith will issue in an arid scholasticism, a joyless rationalism, a dead orthodoxy. It has done so, and it will do so. On the other hand, *my* faith without *the* faith ends up in a sloppy sentimentalism and a groundless subjectivism.

When Timothy was a student at Harvard, he used to walk across what is called "The Yard," the quadrangle in the center of the campus, on his way to the library. Every day he walked past Emerson Hall. Emerson Hall was constructed to house the philosophy department in the early part of the twentieth century. William James, who was the great founder of psychology of religion and an advocate of the philosophy of pragmatism, was appointed to a committee to come up with a saying, a legend, that would be carved in stone across the portal of Emerson Hall. His committee came up with the pre-Socratic maxim, "Man is the measure of all things." But, unbeknownst to William James, Harvard president Charles W. Eliot overrode the committee's recommendation. When it was unveiled, instead of that pre-Socratic maxim, "Man is the measure of all things," people looked up astonished, and William James most of all, to read a verse from Psalm 8: "What is man that thou art mindful of him?" The church's faith is a faith that is rooted in the objectivity of God's revelation in Jesus Christ and in the Holy Scriptures.

The faith of the church can be expressed in many ways, but those expressions must be grounded in the Trinitarian and Christological consensus of the early church. What does it mean to be a confessing Christian? It means that we worship and adore the one and only true and living God, who has forever known himself as the Father, the Son, and the Holy Spirit. We further believe that this triune God of love and holiness became incarnate in Jesus of Nazareth, the Son of Man of the four canonical Gospels. We confess that Jesus Christ is the one and only Lord of heaven and earth. Jesus Christ is the only-begotten Son of God, light from light, true God from true God. This one, we confess, who is the Lord of the church, was miraculously conceived by the Holy Spirit and born of the blessed Virgin Mary; he lived a sinless life, died a sacrificial and substitutionary death on the cross, was buried, is risen and ascended; and he is coming again as the king and judge of all who are, ever were, or ever shall be. Evangelical Protestants, Roman Catholics, and orthodox believers all stand in fundamental continuity with the 318 fathers of Nicaea, the 150 fathers of the First Council of Constantinople, and the canons of Ephesus, including the condemnation of Pelagianism, as well as the affirmations of the Council of Chalcedon (451).[5]

Today, there are some Christians who seek to reclaim the Christian intellectual tradition of the early church by leapfrogging over the Reformation of the sixteenth century. However, to attempt

---

[5]See Thomas C. Oden, *The Rebirth of Orthodoxy* (New York: Harper Collins, 2003).

this is to fail to take seriously what the Reformers themselves said about the catholicity of the church. Hence, confessing Christians are called to affirm both the formal and material principles of the Protestant Reformers. The formal principle, sometimes referred to by the slogan *sola scriptura*, was set forth with clarity by Martin Luther in his famous debate with Johann Eck at Leipzig in 1519 and reiterated in classic form ten years later at the Diet of Speyer, which also gave us the word *Protestant*, understood not in the later sense of "protest against" but rather "witness on behalf of" (*pro-testantes*):

> We are determined by God's grace and aid to abide in God's Word alone, the holy Gospel contained in the biblical books of the Old and New Testaments. This Word alone should be preached, and nothing that is contrary to it. It is the only Truth. It is the sure rule of all Christian doctrine and conduct. It can never fail or deceive us. Who so builds and abides on this foundation shall stand against all the gates of hell, while all merely human editions and vanities set up against it must fall before the presence of God.[6]

The material principle of the Reformation refers to the doctrine of justification by faith alone. Building on the anti-Pelagian thrust of the Augustinian tradition, the Protestant Reformers emphasized that no one can be made righteous before God through the piling up of merits, the intercession of saints, or human works of any kind. Salvation is by grace alone, through faith alone, in Jesus Christ alone. This was not seen as a novel teaching or new doctrine suddenly come to light in the sixteenth century. The Reformers saw themselves in doctrinal continuity with the early church when they set forth the material principle of the Reformation. Jaroslav Pelikan has summarized well the essence of their argument:

> If the Holy Trinity was as holy as the trinitarian dogma taught; if original sin was as virulent as the Augustinian tradition said it was; and if Christ was as necessary as the christological dogma

---

[6]See E. G. Leonard, *History of Protestantism* (Indianapolis: Bobs-Merrill, 1968), 122–28.

implied—then the only way to treat justification in a manner faithful to the best of Catholic tradition was to teach justification by faith.[7]

The heritage of the Fathers and the Reformers must be reclaimed in our own time. What does it mean to be a confessing Christian today?

In 1934, a group of committed Christians, pastors and laity, gathered at a little German town called Barmen, near Düsseldorf. There in the face of the onslaught of what would become the reign of terror of the Third Reich under Adolf Hitler, they issued a declaration of conscience, the Barmen Declaration.[8] This took place after Hitler had come to power and before the "German Christians" had Nazified the church and taken over so many of its offices and prerogatives and when the Aryan paragraph, as they called it, had excluded Jews from the common life of people in Germany—the forerunner to sending them to concentration camps. In 1934, the camp at Dachau had already been built. All this was in the air. Catholicism as a national movement in Germany was sidelined and compromised to some extent by the Concordat the pope had entered into with Hitler. Protestantism and its reigning liberal theology were undermining the witness of the church. In this time of great crisis these Christians gathered and issued the Barmen Declaration, which said: "Jesus Christ, as he is testified to us in the Holy Scripture, is the one Word of God whom we are to hear, whom we are to trust, whom we are to obey in life and in death."[9]

Those who signed that statement, those who drafted it, soon found themselves excluded. Karl Barth, one of the drafters, lost his professorship at the University of Bonn and was sent into exile. Another, Martin Niemöller, was placed in a concentration

---

[7]Jaroslav Pelikan, *Obedient Rebels* (New York: Harper & Row, 1964), 50–51.
[8]The "Theological Declaration of Barmen" was written by Karl Barth and the confessing church in Nazi Germany in opposition to Adolf Hitler's national church. Its central doctrines concern the sin of idolatry and the lordship of Christ, and may be found at http://www.sacred-texts.com/chr/barmen.htm.
[9]Ibid.

camp and became Hitler's private prisoner. Again and again he was interviewed by Hitler, and on one of those occasions he said to Hitler, "You can imprison me and you can torture me and you can kill me, but Herr Hitler, one day you will give an account to one who is the King of kings and the Lord of lords." Where did he get a faith like that? It was not because he was depending on his own private piety or emotions or because he had simply studied theology in a scholastic and academic way, but rather because *the* faith had become *his* faith, and it was the *church's* faith, which is foundational and central to our understanding of the Christian intellectual tradition.

At the end of World War II, Albert Einstein wrote a letter to Martin Niemöller, and this is what he said:

> Having always been an ardent partisan of freedom, I turned to the Universities, as soon as the revolution broke out in Germany, to find the Universities took refuge in silence. I then turned to the editors of powerful newspapers, who, but lately in flowing articles, had claimed to be the faithful champions of liberty. These men, as well as the Universities, were reduced to silence in a few weeks. I then addressed myself to the authors individually, to those who passed themselves off as the intellectual guides of Germany, and among whom many had frequently discussed the question of freedom and its place in modern life. They are in their turn very dumb. Only the church opposed the fight which Hitler was waging against liberty. Till then I had no interest in the Church, but now I feel great admiration and am truly attracted to the Church which had the persistent courage to fight for spiritual truth and moral freedom. I feel obliged to confess that I now admire what I used to consider of little value.[10]

Einstein was driven from Germany because he was a Jew, but it was the church of Jesus Christ, the church's faith put forward in a tumultuous time, that impressed the greatest scientist of the modern world.

---

[10]Ernst C. Helmreich, *The German Churches under Hitler: Background, Struggle, and Epilogue* (Detroit, MI: Wayne State University Press, 1979), 345.

IMPLICATIONS FOR THE CHRISTIAN INTELLECTUAL TRADITION

The shaping of the Christian intellectual tradition in our day calls for a robust recovery of "the faith once delivered to the saints." This does not require that every member of the faculty become an expert in the history of Christian doctrine. Nor does it mean that the discipline of theology must be reinstated as the queen of the sciences. But it does mean that everyone involved in learning, teaching, and research should recognize the biblical narrative and its unfolding in the life of the church as the environment, the *umwelt*, by which his or her specific work and discipline is to be understood and carried out. It is not enough to be a nominal Christian of one type or another, or to pay lip service to the religious mission of an institution in some vague, generic sense. It is not enough to be nice and humane and concerned for those in need. By themselves, such traits, however admirable, will do nothing to pass on the faith intact to the next generation.

Our understanding of the great tradition of Christian thinking is shaped by foundational theological commitments. In addition it is formed by a conviction that faith and reason are mutually illuminating in an uncompromising commitment to truth. Thus the search for truth in any and every discipline can be a sacred activity. Our calling then is to think deeply and clearly about matters of ultimate concern, to love the Lord our God with all our mind, and to invite others to join us on this journey. As we conclude our work in this study guide, we want to take initial steps to show how the work of the Christian intellectual tradition, understood as a sacred endeavor, has been applied in the shaping of educational efforts through the years. Furthermore, we want to make a proposal, suggesting ways that the great tradition of Christian thinking can be advanced for our time. We now move our discussion in that direction.

5

THE APPLICATION AND ADVANCEMENT OF THE GREAT TRADITION

One of the great deficiencies of pietism was the belief that the Christian intellectual tradition could be left behind.

Stanley Hauerwas, *The State of the University* (2007)

We must derive our theory of education from our philosophy of life.

T. S. Eliot, "Modern Education and the Classics" (1932)

Our vision for reclaiming the Christian intellectual tradition is not just about an inward, subjective, personal, and pious Christianity. That would miss the distinctive mission to which Christian educators have been called. The Christian faith is more than a moral code or warm-hearted devotional practices, for the Christian faith influences not only how we act but also what we believe, how we think, how we write, how we teach, how we lead, how we govern, and how we treat one another. While this volume serves as an introduction to the meaning and history of the Christian intellectual tradition, it is our hope that the remaining volumes in the series will enable us to better understand the way the Christian faith has influenced our understanding of literature, history, government, philosophy, art, and moral reasoning among other subjects.

We believe that a better understanding of the Christian intellectual tradition and its application for our various contexts will help us to engage the culture and to prepare a generation of leaders who can effectively serve both church and society. Not only must the Christian intellectual tradition be reclaimed and renewed for our day, but we trust that we can offer ways for it to be advanced and applied. We believe that this tradition can be advanced and applied because of our understanding that humans, created in the image of God, desire to discover truth and that the exploration of truth is possible because the universe, as created by God, is intelligible. These beliefs are held together by our understanding that the unity of knowledge is grounded in our understanding that in Jesus Christ, all things hold together (Col. 1:17). The Christian faith then provides the lens to see the world, recognizing that faith seeks to understand every dimension of life under the lordship of Jesus Christ. It is to a model of such application that we now turn our attention, particularly as it relates to education through the years, a model that we would today call Christian higher education. We look to the past to find guidance for today.[1]

LEARNING CENTERS IN THE EARLY CHURCH

Beginning in the second century, there were important learning centers in Alexandria and Antioch as well as in Constantinople. These centers focused on catechetical and apologetical instruction for Christian converts. While there were differences in approaches as we learned in chapter 1, we can turn to the Alexandrian School to find a model to help us understand the shape of education in the church's early centuries as exemplified in one of the first great Christian scholars, Clement of Alexandria (ca. 150–215). Clement became the leader of the

---

[1] Much of what we are suggesting calls for us to think quite differently from the characteristic way of thinking in our contemporary twenty-first-century world. Thoughtful examples can be found in the essays edited by Robert Kolb, *The American Mind Meets the Mind of Christ* (St. Louis, MO: Concordia Seminary Press, 2010); also guidance can be found in C. S. Lewis, *God in the Dock* (repr. Grand Rapids, MI: Eerdmans, 1994), particularly the chapters "The Transmission of Christianity" and "The Reading of Old Books."

School of Alexandria in 190, a position he held until after the turn of the century when persecution forced him out of Egypt into Cappadocia. His principal literary works produced during this time were a trilogy: *Exhortations*, *Tutor,* and *Miscellanies.* The three works follow a pattern in which, according to Clement, the divine *Logos* first of all converts us (which is the focus of *Exhortation*), then disciplines us (which is the focus of *Tutor*), and finally instructs us (which is the focus of his rather unsystematic work titled *Miscellanies*).[2]

For the most part, Clement's reflections are philosophical, ethical, and even political. His works are grounded in the divine *Logos*, the Word of God who was incarnate in Jesus Christ. Just as Clement looked to the past in drawing from Moses, Israel's great leader, from Plato, the great philosopher, and from Philo, the Jewish philosopher who preceded him, Alexandria, so we today can look to Clement as a source and guide for the challenges of our day. Clement, without compromising the need to analyze and refute aspects of the pagan culture around him, became a master of the philosophical currents of his day.[3] Clement reflected great understanding of Plato and Aristotle. He developed an ambitious and complex philosophical model that mapped out all the sciences and their specialties under the broad headings of theoretical, physical, and natural science.

Clement serves as an instructive guide for us in our context because of his wide range of learning, his love for philosophy and literature, his cultivation of an intellectually serious Christian faith, and his engagement and interaction with trends and issues

---

[2]See David S. Dockery, *Renewing Minds: Serving Church and Society through Christian Higher Education* (Nashville: Broadman, 2008), 52–66; Oliver O'Donovan and Joan Lockwood O'Donovan, *From Irenaeus to Grotius: A Source Book in Christian Political Thought* (Grand Rapids, MI: Eerdmans, 1999), 30–39; R. C. Lilla, *Clement of Alexandria: A Study of Christian Platonism and Gnosticism* (London: Oxford, 1971); David S. Dockery, *Biblical Interpretation Then and Now* (Grand Rapids, MI: Baker, 1992), 82–86.

[3]See O'Donovan, *From Irenaeus to Grotius*, 30–35; Eric F. Osburn, *The Philosophy of Clement of Alexandria* (Cambridge, UK: Cambridge University Press, 1975); James L. Kugel and Rowan A. Greer, *Early Biblical Interpretation* (Philadelphia: Westminster, 1986), 156–99.

of his day. Clement's overarching concern was to develop a view of the world and of life from the vantage point of wisdom in which he understood and interacted with the various strands of thought and culture in his day. Clement's impact as a pioneer of serious Christian thinking cannot be underestimated. Even though his writing was at times unsystematic, he nevertheless presented a coherent and consistent explication of the importance of Christian thinking and ethics for the challenges of his day.

Clement's work also delved into wide-ranging issues such as economics, business, the management of wealth, concern for the poor, and a variety of the social issues of his day. Prior to the time of the Renaissance, he could be characterized as a renaissance person, a singular source for liberal arts thinking. Ultimately, however, Clement was an educator, taking seriously his calling as a teacher. His favorite designation was *Tutor* (*Paidagogos*), the title of his middle work.

His appreciation for art and music provided opportunity for his interaction with the arts of the third century. Clement's writings pointed to Christ as most noble minstrel while observing that men and women are the harp and lyre. Clement's work contrasted the beauty of Christianity with hopelessness of pagan poetry and philosophy. Ultimately Clement pointed to the source of all life in God by maintaining that men and women are born for God. Full or ultimate truth, Clement claimed, is found in Christ alone.[4] Clement prepared the way for the educational advancements in the thought of Augustine.

AUGUSTINE TO AQUINAS: THE MEDIEVAL PERIOD

Augustine, the father of the Christian intellectual tradition, located the source of knowledge within the person, based on his understanding that truth was a gift of God's grace granted through faith. This knowledge, or potential knowledge, is developed by

---

[4]Paul Avis, *The History of Christian Theology*, 3 vols. (Grand Rapids, MI: Eerdmans, 1988), 25–30.

education that actively works in and through reason, memory, and will. Education takes place by engaging the Christian tradition,[5] the wisdom of the ages that enabled the development of the liberal arts tradition.[6] Augustine encouraged personal discovery and active engagement of students in the disciplines of study. For Augustine, the love for learning reflects our desire for God, and the love for wisdom exemplifies loving God with our minds in fulfillment of the Great Commandment (Matt. 22:37–39).

Eight centuries later, Thomas Aquinas emphasized sense experience as the primary source of knowledge. While Augustine's approach to education was influenced by Plato, Aquinas was partial to Aristotle. For Aquinas, reason reflects on the data of the senses, for nothing is ever in the mind that is not first in the senses. Reason enables understanding and discernment, informing the will and giving guidance for life. Aquinas favored a teacher-centered, didactic approach to education.[7]

During the medieval period, Christian education flourished in the monastery. The monastic educational model emphasized a life of study, prayer, meditation, and work. The curriculum was built around the study of Holy Scripture, particularly the Psalms, and the rule of faith as articulated in the Apostles' Creed and Nicene Creed. Reading, writing, grammar, and music were also included, forming the trajectory for the trivium (grammar, rhetoric, and dialectic) and the quadrivium (arithmetic, geometry, music, and astronomy). The trivium and quadrivium, the core of the liberal arts curriculum, were significant for shaping the cathedral school and medieval university. Philosophy, physics, ethics, and ultimately

---

[5]See G. R. Evans, "Tradition," in *Augustine through the Ages: An Encyclopedia*, ed. Allan D. Fitzgerald (Grand Rapids, MI: Eerdmans, 1999), 842–43.
[6]See Mark W. Roche, *The Intellectual Appeal of Catholicism and the Idea of a Catholic University* (Notre Dame, IN: University of Notre Dame Press, 2003); also John Mark Reynolds, *When Athens Met Jerusalem* (Downers Grove, IL: InterVarsity, 2009).
[7]See Joseph Wawrykow, "Thomas Aquinas," in *Augustine through the Ages*, 829–32.

theology, the queen of the sciences, completed the studies for students in the medieval universities.[8]

REFORMATION AND POST-REFORMATION

The contribution of Desiderius Erasmus to education can be characterized as the work of an innovative pioneer moving beyond tradition and supplying impetus for Reformation and post-Reformation studies. His brilliance and courage paved the way for the direction of Christian education for the decades that followed. A prince among the Renaissance humanists, Erasmus was at the same time a conceptual and reforming theologian. A scholarly biblical critic and pious moralist, Erasmus offered multiple contributions to education worthy of appreciation. He was the premier Renaissance scholar with an emphasis on the original sources and the study of ancient texts.

Erasmus made an important break with the medieval scholastic approach to theology and the study of Scripture, but not in a reactionary manner. The break came about through a combination of Christian commitment, Renaissance scholarship, and the implementation of John Colet's educational model. The genius and ability of Erasmus as biblical scholar and moral theologian served as a model for Luther, Melanchthon, Calvin, and other Reformers.[9]

Martin Luther and Philip Melanchthon shaped education in Germany in the sixteenth century with their emphasis on the priesthood of all believers, which not only encouraged Bible reading for all but also stressed literacy and education for all. Melanchthon, more than Luther, shaped educational theory as a leader at Wittenberg University. As the curriculum

---

[8]See Edward Farley, *Theologia: The Fragmentation and Unity of Theological Education* (Philadelphia: Fortress, 1983); David Kelsey, *To Understand God Truly: What Is Theological about a Theological School* (Louisville: Westminster, 1992).

[9]This section has been adapted from David S. Dockery, "The Foundation of Reformation Hermeneutics: A Fresh Look at Erasmus," in *Evangelical Hermeneutics*, ed. Michael Bauman and David Hall (Camp Hill, PA: Christian Publications, 1995).

organizer and systematizer of theology, Melanchthon was known as the *Praeceptor Germaniae*. His work brought about significant changes in the German educational system.

Post-Reformation educational models led to the rise of the modern university at the University of Halle (1694). Halle began as an educational center focused on serious study coupled with warm-hearted piety, in reaction to the rationalistic scholasticism that characterized some aspects of the post-Reformation period. Soon, however, the educational agenda was dominated by Enlightenment priorities.[10] Higher education for the past three hundred years has lived with the tension of post-Enlightenment philosophies such as rationalism, empiricism, existentialism, phenomenology, and Marxist and recent radical feminist epistemologies. For these reasons, among others, Christian higher education today needs to reclaim and advance the Christian intellectual tradition. The University of Halle provided the first example, of many that have followed, where piety alone was not able in and of itself to sustain the great tradition of Christian thinking.

RENEWED VISION FOR CHRISTIAN HIGHER EDUCATION

The confessional foundation, the rule of faith, identified in previous chapters will serve us well as we consider a proposal for renewed vision for Christian higher education. We want to begin with an affirmation of the Apostles' Creed, and from there cultivate a holistic orthodoxy based on a high view of Scripture that is congruent with the great affirmations of the early church regarding the holy Trinity. We need to find ways to avoid falling into the ditch on the left side (liberalism) or the right side (fundamentalism) of the road, which, unfortunately, when looking at history, seems all too easy to do. By reconnecting with the great *consensus*

---

[10]See David S. Dockery, "New Testament Interpretation: A Historical Survey," in *New Testament Criticism and Interpretation*, ed. D. A. Black and David S. Dockery (Grand Rapids, MI: Zondervan, 1991), 41–72.

fidei, the great confessional tradition of the church, we can help prevent falling into fundamentalist reductionism on the one hand or liberal revisionism on the other.[11] A resistance to both reductionism and revisionism, while adopting an openness to imaginative thought, will help us appropriately see things in terms of both/and (*religio et eruditio*) rather than either/or.

TRINITARIAN FAITH

We need to recognize that in essentials of the Trinitarian faith, there is no place for compromise. Faith and truth are primary issues, and Christian colleges and universities must stand firm in those areas. Faith and truth are primary, and we may not appeal to love or grace as an excuse to deny any essential aspect of Christian teaching. By connecting with the Christian intellectual tradition and the great confessional tradition, we can find guidance and insight to help navigate our way in the unchartered waters we will face in the future. Historical awareness, knowledge of the past, will help us avoid confusing what is merely a momentary expression from that which has enduring importance.

THE UNIVERSITY AT THE HEART OF THE CHURCH: *EX CORDE ECCLESIAE*

A renewed vision for Christian higher education must also encourage a connection to the churches. James Burtchaell, in his important work *The Dying of the Light*, surveyed dozens of institutions across various traditions, focusing on nineteenth- and twentieth-century examples. Burtchaell suggested that when the disconnection with the churches took place, the light of the Christian faith began to die on these campuses.[12] Christian colleges and universi-

---

[11]Aspects of this proposal can be found in Dockery, *Renewing Minds*; and David S. Dockery, *Southern Baptist Consensus and Renewal* (Nashville: Broadman, 2009), 134–67.

[12]See James T. Burtchaell, *The Dying of the Light: The Disengagement of Colleges and Universities from Their Churches* (Grand Rapids, MI: Eerdmans, 1998); also John J. Piderit, "The University at the Heart of the Church," *First Things* (June/July 1999): 22–25. The review of the Burtchaell volume by Michael Beaty provides a most insightful guide. The review can be found in *The Journal*

ties must not be confused with churches, yet they are an extension of the churches, the academic arm of the kingdom of God.

The challenge is for Christian universities to stay connected to the confessional heritage found in the heart of the churches so as to pass on the Christian tradition, while encouraging honest intellectual inquiry. We need to affirm the great tradition of Christian thinking while encouraging genuine intellectual engagement in the areas of teaching, research, and scholarship. There is no place for anti-intellectualism on Christian university campuses. Christian higher education has been called to be academically rigorous, grounded in the Christian intellectual tradition epitomized by Clement of Alexandria, Augustine, and dozens of others. Students and faculty at Christian universities need to develop the kind of intellectual curiosity and imagination that seeks to understand the great ideas of history while engaging the issues of today.

OPENNESS TO INTELLECTUAL INQUIRY

We want to encourage genuine exploration and serious research on Christian university campuses while recognizing that free inquiry, untethered to tradition or to the church, often results in the unbelieving skepticism that has characterized large sectors of higher education since the Enlightenment.[13] The directionless state that can be seen as we look across much of higher education has often taken place because many former church-related institutions have become disconnected from the churches and their tradition. Therefore, a renewed vision for Christian higher education is needed to help develop unifying principles for Christian thinking, founded on the tenet that all truth has its source in God, our creator and our redeemer.

---

of College and University Law 27:177. Gary Parrett and Steve Kang have proposed ways that the churches can strengthen their own educational efforts. See Parrett and Kang, *Teaching the Faith, Forming the Faithful* (Downers Grove, IL: InterVarsity, 2009).

[13]See Anthony T. Diekema, *Academic Freedom and Christian Scholarship* (Grand Rapids, MI: Eerdmans, 2000).

As we do so, we will struggle with many issues, because there are many issues for which we still see through a glass darkly, issues that are filled with ambiguities. Some questions will have to remain unanswered as we continue to struggle and wrestle together. Yet we envision a distinctive approach to teaching and learning.

AN AWARENESS OF CHALLENGES
FROM VARIOUS DIRECTIONS

We must not fail to recognize the challenges we will face in this journey, both from the academy and the culture, as well as from the church.[14] There are those in the churches who would be satisfied if church-related institutions merely provided a place for warm-hearted piety that would encourage campus ministry and mission trips. The mission of Christian higher education must include more than the promotion of piety and activism. Christian universities must give priority to Christian thinking and thinking Christianly, learning to think carefully, critically, and creatively, engaging the culture and the academy, or, to borrow the phrase from T. S. Eliot, "to think in Christian categories."[15] Thus we must seek to build Christian universities that are faithful to the lordship of Christ; that exemplify the Great Commandment; that seek justice, mercy, and love; that demonstrate responsible freedom; that prioritize worship and service as central to all pursuits in life.

We recognize that a commitment to academic excellence is best demonstrated by quality students and teaching. Research and teaching, faithful to the Christian intellectual tradition, will be prioritized and emphasized. We must bring students to a mature reflection of what the Christian faith means for every field of study.

---

[14]See Phil Eaton, *Engaging the Culture, Changing the World: The Christian University in a Post-Christian World* (Downers Grove, IL: InterVarsity, 2011); also see David S. Dockery, "Blending Baptist with Orthodox in the Christian University," in *The Future of Baptist Higher Education,* ed. Donald Schmeltekopf and Dianna Vitanza (Waco, TX: Baylor University Press, 2006).
[15]T. S. Eliot, *Christianity and Culture* (New York: Harcourt Brace, 1940), 22.

In doing so we can help develop a grace-filled convictional community of learning. We are, however, also constantly reminded that we live in a fallen world, and, thus, at times the best we can do is to see in a mirror dimly (1 Cor. 13:12).

All faculty members at Christian universities have the privilege and responsibility to pass on the Christian intellectual tradition as it informs and influences all the various disciplines. We believe such a responsibility to teach, inform, and communicate in a manner faithful to this tradition is possible because all human beings, everywhere and at all times, are made in the image of God. Such a commitment helps to shape a shared community where we learn from one another and seek to engage all peoples, cultures, and traditions in genuine conversation.

Because we can think, relate, and communicate in understandable words, and since men and women have been created in the image of God, we can creatively teach, learn, explore, carry on research, and pass along the best aspects of the Christian intellectual tradition. Thus, we want to maintain that there is a complementary place for teaching and scholarship, for service and research. A Christian university, in common with any other institution of higher learning, must surely subordinate all other endeavors to the improvement of the mind in pursuit of truth. Yet the Christian intellectual tradition has not been and is not limited to a focus on the mind, the mastery of content. For though these things are primary, they are not enough. We believe that character development and faith formation, in addition to guidance in professional competencies, are also to be considered significant. Furthermore, we think the pursuit of truth is best undertaken within a community of learning that includes colleagues of the present and voices from the past, "the communion of saints," who have shaped what we know as the Christian intellectual tradition. In doing so, we propose a vision for a holistic approach to education that attends to the moral, spiritual, physical, and social development of its students following the pattern of Jesus, who himself increased in wisdom and stature, and in favor with God and with others (Luke 2:52).

As Mark Noll has reminded us in his introduction to *The Christian College: A History of Protestant Higher Education in America*, it has been theological seminaries, more so than Christian universities, that have remained the most successful institutions for advancing the study of the Christian intellectual tradition. He noted that the work from the Protestant seminaries has produced some of the most significant and vibrant Christian publications that retain their intellectual weight and cultural breadth, doing so well into the twentieth century. In fact, he noted that even into the twenty-first century "professors at evangelical seminaries are still the best trained of all professional academics identified with evangelical institutions, and their work is read far more widely in evangelical circles than work from professors in the Christian colleges."[16]

APPLYING THE TRADITION IN THE CONTEXT OF CHRISTIAN UNIVERSITIES

This raises the question of the place of the Christian intellectual tradition among the Christian colleges and universities. It has become clear over the past fifty years, in particular, that the serious work and Christian commentary on the arts, humanities, sciences, social sciences, public ethics, and professional studies has taken place at the colleges and universities. It is all the more reason for the Christian intellectual tradition to be reclaimed by Christian scholars in all of these fields. It is time to ask important questions about the role of faith and reason, Christian worldview and learning, Scripture and the disciplines.

The challenges facing Christian colleges and universities cannot be neutralized simply by adding nicer facilities, better

---

[16]Mark Noll, "Introduction," in William C. Ringenberg, *The Christian College: A History of Protestant Higher Education in America*, 2nd ed. (Grand Rapids, MI: Baker, 2006), 17–36.

campus-ministry opportunities, and improved student-life programs, as important as these things are. Our twenty-first-century context must again recognize the importance of serious Christian thinking and confessional orthodoxy as both necessary and appropriate for the well-being of Christian academic communities. If the Christian faith is to regain a voice in the academy and in the public square, it must rediscover what G. K. Chesterton (1874–1936) termed the "romance of orthodoxy."[17] Chesterton set forth his appeal not only on the grounds of Christianity's truth claims but also on Christianity's capacity to answer the human need for an active and imaginative life, picturesque and full of poetical curiosity. On this path we invite others to travel. We offer the Christian intellectual tradition to twenty-first-century Christ followers as a guide to truth, to that which is imaginatively compelling, emotionally engaging, aesthetically enhancing, and personally liberating.[18]

The Christian intellectual tradition has been shaped by history and philosophy, Scripture and theology, but we believe it has bearing on every subject and academic discipline in the modern university. While at times the Christian's research in any field might follow similar paths and methods as the secularists, doxology at both the beginning and end of research marks the work of believers from that of secularists.[19] It is generally no small secret that Christian thinking is no longer considered a necessary subject in the modern university. Perhaps it is allowed in history or religion departments, where one can report on what was once believed by Christians. Thus, we recognize that our proposal might be considered "outrageous" by some.[20]

We want to introduce students to Christian thinkers in all

[17]See G. K. Chesterton, *Orthodoxy* (repr. New York: Doubleday, 1959), 129–47.

[18]See William Lynch, *Christ and Apollo* (Notre Dame, IN: University of Notre Dame Press, 1960); Alister McGrath, *A Scientific Theology*, vol. 3 (London: T&T Clark, 2003), 3–76; Alister McGrath, *Heresy* (San Francisco: HarperOne, 2009), 232–34.

[19]See Mark Noll, "Reconsidering Christendom," in *The Future of Christian Learning*, ed. Thomas A. Howard (Grand Rapids, MI: Brazos, 2008), 23–70.

[20]See George M. Marsden, *The Outrageous Idea of Christian Scholarship* (New York: Oxford University Press, 2002).

disciplines who have helped to shape this wonderful tradition. The list not only includes the scholars identified in our previous chapters, but also William Wilberforce, G. K. Chesterton, T. S. Eliot, Dorothy Sayers, C. S. Lewis, Johann Sebastian Bach, George Frideric Handel, Sir William Blackstone, Isaac Newton, Johannes Kepler, Louis Pasteur, Venerable Bede, Booker T. Washington, George Washington Carver, Peter Akinola, Henry Luke Orombi, Elizabeth Fox-Genovese, and on and on we could go.

The pursuit of the greater glory of God remains rooted in a Christian worldview in which God can be encountered in the search for truth in every discipline. The application of the Christian intellectual tradition will encourage members of Christian university communities to see their teaching, research, study, student formation, administrative service, and trustee guidance within the framework of the gospel of Jesus Christ. In such a context scholars will see their scholarship as contributing to the unity of knowledge. Professors and students will help to enhance a love for learning that encourages a life of worship and service. The great tradition of Christian thinking helps all of us better see the relationship between the Christian faith and the role of reason, while encouraging Christ followers to seek truth and engage the culture, with a view toward strengthening the church and extending the kingdom of God.

CONCLUSION

An attempt to apply and advance the Christian intellectual tradition invites those involved in Christian higher education to be unapologetically Christian and rigorously academic. It means developing resources for serious Christian thinking and scholarship in all disciplines, not just theology, biblical studies, philosophy, and history. In order to reclaim, renew, and advance the breadth and depth of this marvelous tradition, we must have at least a basic awareness and understanding of it, which is the purpose for this entire series.

We believe the time is right to reconsider afresh this tradition because of the challenges and disorder across the academic spectrum. The reality of the fallen world in which we live is magnified for us in day-to-day life through broken families, confusion in the area of sexuality, conflicts between nations, and the racial and ethnic prejudice we observe all around us.

The Christian intellectual tradition offers a distinctive and hopeful vision, helping us to understand that there is a place for music and the arts because God is the God of creation and beauty. We recognize that the social sciences can make observations to strengthen society, families, and religious structures by recognizing the presence of the image of God in all men and women. Those who study economics can help address problems facing communities and society at large, as well as expand our awareness of how wealth is produced and how good stewardship calls for it to be used. Political philosophy scholars can strategize about ways to address issues of government, public policy, war, justice, and peace. Ethical challenges in business, education, and health care can be illuminated by reflection on the great tradition.

While there is no corner of the modern university to which the Christian faith is indifferent, we need to recognize that not every subject is equally affected by such distinctive Christian thinking. Mathematics and computer science will perhaps be less impacted than philosophy, the arts, or the social sciences. Exploring every discipline from the confessional perspective that "we believe in God, the Father Almighty, maker of heaven and earth" will, however, both shape and sharpen our focus. When foundational commitments play a more obvious role, recognition of the influence of the Christian intellectual tradition will become more important. We want to invite Christian scholars to embrace truth where it is made known or discovered, following the lead of Cardinal Newman, who proposed that all that is good or true or beautiful or beneficent, be it great, small, perfect, fragmentary, natural, supernatural, moral, or material, finds its source and meaning in God.[21] This proposal is rooted in the conviction that God, the source of all truth, has revealed himself fully in Jesus Christ, and it is in our belief in the union of the divine and human in Jesus Christ where the unity of truth will ultimately be seen.

We recognize the insufficiencies of the following movements to provide guidance for this lofty proposal: (1) popular Christianity, with its imbalanced emphasis on activism and its suspicion of the intellectual; (2) liberalism, with its misguided redefinitions of the Christian faith; (3) pietism, with its separation of "head" from "heart"; and (4) fundamentalism, with its separatistic and legalistic strictures. These four responses are incomplete, imbalanced, and at times distorted and incoherent. What is needed is a renewed understanding and appreciation of the depth and breadth of the Christian intellectual tradition, with its commitments to the church's historic confession of the Trinitarian God, and an understanding of the world and all subject matter as fully understandable only in relation to this Trinitarian God.

Ultimately, we recognize all knowledge has its source in God. We want to respond rightly to this recognition by loving God with all our minds and by promoting intellectual seriousness and intellectual curiosity among our students. We desire to avoid the pitfalls of disciplinary "overspecialization," while seeking to interact with issues and trends in our changing world. We are excited to think that this changing twenty-first-century world is likely to bring new global partners for this effort.

We rejoice to think that seeking to reclaim the Christian intellectual tradition will promote faithful Christian confessionalism while encouraging authentic inquiry within this confessional context. We confess our belief that God has revealed himself to us in creation, in history, in our conscience, and ultimately in Jesus Christ

---

[21]See John Henry Newman, *The Idea of a University* (repr. London: Longman, Green, 1907); also Noll, "Reconsidering Christendom," 23–70.

(Col. 1:15–18). This God-revealed truth provides the framework for understanding and interpreting the world, the events of human history, and our responsibilities toward God and one another. It is our hope that as we wrestle with the great ideas of history and the pressing issues of our day that the great tradition of Christian thinking will provide both the resources and the examples to encourage our faith and shape significant intellectual pursuits, even as we value the life of the mind for the glory of God. While our approach to higher education values and prioritizes the life of the mind, it is a holistic call for the engagement of head, heart, and hands.

We believe that drawing on the work of those who have gone before us enables us to learn from models of rigorous scholarship (and, as we have seen, also learning negative lessons from those outside the tradition of orthodoxy) while emphasizing the uniqueness and dignity of each student. We trust that knowledge informed by faith will lead to an ethic and formation of character that will serve individuals, families, and churches and promote integrity, justice, and generosity. Not only do we wish to see individuals, families, and churches strengthened; we want to see Christian institutions of higher education strengthened in order to engage the culture and improve society. We long to see fidelity in the life and teaching of these institutions that will help to cultivate a love for the gospel of Jesus Christ.

It is our hope that the ideals and commitments called for in this little volume are not culturally confined, for we believe that these are things that cannot be easily expunged without great peril to ourselves personally and to Christian institutions of higher education corporately, both in the present and in the future. In the midst of a confused culture and the postmodern ethos of our day, we need commitments that are firm but loving, clear but gracious, encouraging the people of God to be ready to respond to the numerous issues and challenges that will come our way, without getting drawn into every intramural squabble in the church or in the culture.

Finally, we invite our readers to join with us in asking God to renew our vision for the Christian academic context, including centers of learning, schools, colleges, universities, and seminaries. We want to encourage these institutions to recommit themselves to academic excellence in teaching and scholarship, in research and service, and in personal discipleship and churchmanship. We believe this vision can best be implemented by laying hold of the best of the Christian intellectual tradition and carrying it forward with faithfulness for years and decades to come. We gladly join hands together with those who desire to join us on this journey, seeking the good of all concerned as we serve together for the glory of our great God.[22] We conclude with the famous words from Bernard of Clairvaux in the twelfth century, words that provide illumination for Christian educators who desire to adopt the great tradition of Christian thinking as a framework for the educational process:

> Some seek knowledge for
> The sake of knowledge;
> That is curiosity;
> Others seek knowledge so that
> They themselves may be known;
> That is vanity;
> But there are still others
> Who seek knowledge in
> Order to serve and edify others;
> And that is charity.[23]

---

[22]In many ways this work extends our previous joint efforts. See David S. Dockery and Timothy George, *Theologians of the Baptist Tradition* (Nashville: Broadman, 2001); and *Building Bridges* (Nashville: Convention, 2007). Similarly, it brings together much of David's previous work regarding Christian higher education. See David S. Dockery, *Shaping a Christian Worldview: Foundation for Christian Higher Education* (Nashville: Broadman, 2002); *Renewing Minds*; *Christian Leadership Essentials: A Handbook for Managing Christian Organizations* (Nashville: Broadman, 2011); and *Faith and Learning: A Handbook for Christian Higher Education* (Nashville: Broadman, 2012).

[23]See F. R. Evans, *Bernard of Clairvaux: Selected Works* (Mahwah, NJ: Paulist Press, 1987).

QUESTIONS FOR REFLECTION

1) How will thinking carefully about the relationship of faith and knowledge influence the way you think about and live out your Christian commitments? Is it important to reflect on these things? Why or why not?

2) How can attempts to reclaim the Christian intellectual tradition address the rapid gains of secularism in the twenty-first century?

3) How will a better understanding of the history of the Christian intellectual tradition provide insight for the teaching/learning process in churches and in Christian academic communities?

4) How has the Christian intellectual tradition been shaped by the Bible and by the interpretation of the Bible?

5) What is meant by phrases such as "the integration of faith and knowledge," "faith and reason," and "faith and learning"? How does your understanding of the Christian intellectual tradition inform and influence your understanding of these phrases?

TIMELINE

Early Church

Year	Person	Events
30–100	Clement of Rome	
35–117	Ignatius of Antioch	
64		Great fire of Rome
70		Fall of Jerusalem
69–160	Polycarp	
85–160	Marcion	
100–120		Didache
100–165	Justin Martyr	
130–202	Irenaeus	
150–215	Clement of Alexandria	School of Alexandria
160–220	Tertullian	
185–254	Origen	
250–336	Arius	
296–373	Athanasius	
312–313		Constantine becomes emperor; Christianity is legalized.
325		Council of Nicaea
329–379	Basil of Caesarea	
330–389	Gregory of Nazianzus	
330–395	Gregory of Nyssa	
341–420	Jerome	
350–428	Theodore of Mopsuestia	School of Antioch
354–407	John Chrysostom	
354–420	Pelagius	
354–430	Augustine	
381		Council of Constantine
410		Rome sacked by Goths
431		Council of Ephesus
451		Council of Chalcedon

Medieval Period

Year	Person	Events
673–735	Venerable Bede	
1033–1109	Anselm	
1054		Great church schism between East and West
1079–1142	Abelard	
1090–1153	Bernard of Clairvaux	
1140–1218	Peter Waldo	
1182–1226	Francis of Assisi	
1225–1274	Thomas Aquinas	
1330–1384	John Wycliffe	
1373–1415	Jon Hus	
1378–1417		Great schism of the papacy
1452–1498	Girolamo Savonarola	
1466–1519	John Colet	
1466–1536	Desiderius Erasmus	
1516		Erasmus edition of Greek New Testament

Reformation Period

Year	Person	Events
1483–1546	Martin Luther	
1484–1531	Ulrich Zwingli	
1497–1560	Philipp Melanchthon	
1509–1564	John Calvin	
1517		Luther nailed ninety-five theses to Wittenberg church door

Post-Reformation Period

Year	Person	Events
1694		University of Halle
1703–1758	Jonathan Edwards	
1703–1791	John Wesley	
1768–1834	Friederich Schleiermacher	
1801–1890	John Henry Cardinal Newman	
1836–1921	A. H. Strong	
1837–1920	Abraham Kuyper	
1851–1921	B. B. Warfield	
1874–1936	G. K. Chesterton	
1886–1968	Karl Barth	
1898–1963	C. S. Lewis	
1913–2003	Carl F. H. Henry	
1931–	Thomas Oden	
1934–		Barmen Declaration
1990–		*Ex Corde Ecclesiae*, Pope John Paul II

GLOSSARY

Alexandrian School. Alexandria was a center of great learning. Here Philo developed his allegorical hermeneutics. The school of thought represented in Alexandria had streams of Platonic, Neoplatonic, and Gnostic thought, and these streams of thought influenced the way Judaism and Christianity were articulated. At the beginning of the third century AD Alexandria became important as a seat of Christian theology. The school was characterized by its dependence upon Neoplatonic philosophy and its application on the allegorical method of biblical interpretation.

Allegorical Interpretation. The approach to interpretation that assumes the text says or intends to say something other than its literal wording suggests. It seeks to draw out a deeper, mystical sense not derivable from the words themselves.

Anagogical Interpretation. A method of biblical interpretation that seeks to unfold the spiritual meaning of a Scripture passage as it relates to eternal or future realities.

Antiochene School. A school of biblical interpretation and theology popular from the third to the eighth centuries AD that developed in Antioch of Syria. The approach tended to be rational, historical, and literal, in contrast to that which had previously developed in Alexandria. Interpreters who followed this approach seemed to be quite methodical, with dependence upon Aristotle and that philosophical tradition.

Apostolic Fathers. A group of early Christian writers believed to have had direct contact with the apostles of the early church. The term is used to describe the earliest noncanonical writings of the late first and early second centuries.

Aristotelianism. A tradition of philosophy based on the teaching of Aristotle, with an emphasis on knowledge that can be acquired through the senses and the exercise of reason.

Arius/Arianism. Arius (250–336) was an elder in an urban parish in Alexandria. Arius taught that God the Father alone is God. This God could not possibly have communicated his essence to any other; thus the Son is a being created by the will and power of the Father. Unlike the Father, Jesus was not without beginning. Arianism was declared to be heretical at both the Council of Nicaea (325) and the Council of Constantinople (381).

Authoritative Hermeneutics. A way of interpreting Scripture to point out the false beliefs of heretics. This was accomplished by establishing the correct theological meaning of Scripture by the authority of the bishop or the rule of faith (*regula fidei*).

Canon/Canonical. The term *canon* refers to the group of books recognized by the early church as sacred Scripture. The Christian canon consists of sixty-six books (thirty-nine Old Testament and twenty-seven New Testament) and eighty books for Catholics, whose canon includes fourteen apocryphal books.

Chalcedon/Chalcedonian Christology. The belief about Jesus Christ adopted at the Council of Chalcedon (451) and considered as the foundation of classical orthodox Christology. The confession affirms Jesus as the one and the same Christ, Son, Lord, Only Begotten to be acknowledged in two natures, without confusion, without change, without division, without separation; the distinction of the natures being in no way abolished because of the union but rather the characteristic property of each one being preserved and concurring into one person and one being.

Christological Interpretation. The Greek word *Christos* (Christ) means "anointed one" and is the equivalent of the Hebrew *Mashiah* (Messiah). Christological interpretation reads the Old Testament in light of the belief that Jesus of Nazareth is the Messiah/Christ and the fulfillment of the Old Testament promises and prophecies.

Christology. The word refers to the teaching of and about Christ, his person and natures. In earlier times, Christology also included the work of Christ, now often treated under the doctrine of salvation.

Confessional Christian Faith. The importance of a full assent to the teachings of the Christian faith by individuals, by churches, and by groups or denominations. A confession of faith by a group or a denomination helps to define and to defend their basic beliefs and identity. The terms *confessions* and *creeds* (such as the Apostles' Creed or the Nicene Creed) are at times used interchangeably, but generally creedalism, as distinct from confessionalism, implies giving the same authority to a creed as is given to Holy Scripture. Historically, evangelical Protestants are best understood to be "a confessional people" rather than "a creedal people."

Consensus Fidei. A Latin term used to describe the consensus of beliefs held by major sectors of the church, the pattern of Christian truth, which has been believed or accepted as orthodox teaching by Christians throughout the centuries.

Early Church. A rather broad and somewhat ambiguous term used to describe the Christian church from Pentecost through its development in the first five centuries. Sometimes the terms *earliest church*, *earliest Christianity*, *primitive church*, or *primitive Christianity* are more focused on the first-century church.

Enlightenment Philosophy. A philosophical movement during the seventeenth and eighteenth centuries, sometimes identified as the Age of Reason. Characterized by rationalism and self-sufficiency, it rejected external authorities such as the Bible, tradition, church, or state.

Ex Corde Ecclesia. A Latin phrase that means "born from the heart of the church." It is often used to stress the connectedness of the Christian university to the church.

Formal Principle of Theology. A term that refers to the authority that forms or shapes the doctrine being considered. For evangelical Protestants, a reference to the formal principle points to Scripture as a primary authority and to tradition (or experience or reason) as a secondary authority. *Formal principle* is often used in contrast with the term *material principle*, which refers to the matter or central teaching of Christian belief.

Functional Hermeneutics. A way of describing how readers apply the biblical text to their own context and situation without attention to its original context or situation. Meaning is thus bound up with Scripture's functional application.

General Revelation. God's self-disclosure in a general way to all people at all times in all places. God reveals himself through nature, history, human experience, and human conscience.

Gnosticism. A group of mystery religions that developed in the late second century, a radical dualistic aberration of Christian teaching concerning God and the world.

Hermeneutics. From the Greek *hermeneuein:* to express, to explain, to translate, to interpret. It is variously defined but refers to a theory of interpretation. Traditionally, hermeneutics has sought to establish the principles, methods, and rules needed for the interpretation of written texts, particularly sacred texts.

Inerrancy. The idea that, when all the facts are known, the Bible (in its original writings), properly interpreted in light of the culture and the means of communication that had developed by the time of its composition, will be found to be completely true in all that it affirms, to the degree of precision intended by the author's purpose, in all matters relating to God and his creation.

Infallibility. The view that the Bible is incapable of error and cannot deceive or mislead.

Inspiration. The work of the Holy Spirit in superintending the biblical writings so that the acts and interpretation of God's revelation have been recorded as God so desired, so that the Bible is actually the written word of God.

Judaizers. A party of Jewish Christians in the early church who taught that observance of the Mosaic law was necessary for salvation.

Late Judaism. Judaism from the closing of the Old Testament canon to the third century AD, specifically its different groups (Pharisees, Sadducees, Essenes, and Zealots) during the intertestamental period and the first century AD.

Literal Interpretation. An attempt to understand Scripture in its plain and ordinary sense without seeing a deeper or spiritual meaning.

Manichaeism. A third-century Gnostic heresy based on the teachings of Mani (ca. 216–276) that emphasized an elaborate cosmology attempting to describe good and evil and light and darkness in the material world. The teachings are similar to Zoroastrianism.

Marcion/Marcionism. A movement in the early church based on the teachings of Marcion (ca. 85–160), a second-century heretic. Marcion rejected the Old Testament and issued his own New Testament consisting of an abbreviated Gospel of Luke (without birth narratives) and ten letters of Paul (excluding the Pastorals). Marcion set forth a stark and unbridgeable contrast between the God of the Old Testament and the Christ of the New Testament.

Medieval Period. Historical period between the fifth and fifteenth centuries.

Midrash. Jewish interpretation of Scripture; more precisely, a commentary that contemporizes Scripture for current and practical situations.

Montanism. A heterodox movement associated with second-century Christianity, based on the teachings of Montanus, which emphasized prophetic teachings from spontaneous and direct inspiration of the Holy Spirit.

Neoplatonism. A term used to describe third-century religious and mystical philosophy that attempted to shape Christian doctrine with interpretations based on the teachings of Plato and the earlier Platonists.

Nicaea/Nicene Christology. The teaching of the fourth-century church derived from the Council of Nicaea (325) and confirmed at Constantinople (381). This teaching was articulated primarily by Athanasius (297–373). The Council of Nicaea condemned Arius by insisting that the Son was not simply the "firstborn of all creation" but was indeed "of one essence with the Father." Against Arius, Athanasius sought to uphold the unity of essence of the Father and Son by basing his argument not on a philosophical doctrine of the nature of the *Logos* but on the nature of the redemption accomplished by the Word in the flesh. Only God himself, taking on human flesh and dying and rising in human flesh, can effect a redemption that consists of being saved from sin and corruption and death and of being raised to share the nature of God himself. After Nicaea, it became apparent that there were two main schools of thought in the church, centered in Alexandria and Antioch respectively. In doctrinal terms, Alexandria claims priority, and Antioch is probably best regarded as a correction of what were believed to be the excesses in Alexandrian thought.

Patristics/the Fathers. The outstanding thinkers and theologians of the first six centuries of the church have come to be regarded as "the Fathers," and the study of these leaders is known as "Patristics."

Pelagius/Pelagianism. Pelagius (ca. 354–440), who lived at the time of Jerome and Augustine (fourth and fifth centuries), taught that good deeds shaped by personal asceticism could produce salvation. For Pelagius, faith was understood in light of the human will's ability to live in a sinless manner. Grace was seen as a blessing of God, an added advantage to rigorous and faithful living. Pelagianism was condemned as a heresy at the Councils of Carthage (416 and 418) and at the Council of Ephesus (431). Though condemned as heresy nearly sixteen hundred years ago, the residual influence of Pelagianism has continued to cause challenges throughout Christian history.

Platonism. A philosophical system founded on the teachings of Plato, with an emphasis on true knowledge based on the ideal forms, the unchangeable perfect forms. Particular objects, which can be known or experienced by the senses, are imperfect copies. Platonism is sometimes called "Platonic idealism" because Plato taught that ideas are ultimately real. Thus, a distinction between the ideal and nonideal realm must be maintained.

Postmodernism. Describes a time and a dislocating of the human condition in the early years of the twenty-first century. Postmodernism impacts literature, art, dress, architecture, music, self-identity, ethics, and theology. Postmodernism tends to view human experience as incoherent, lacking absolutes or a metanarrative for truth, meaning, or morals. This way of viewing the world presents Christians with new challenges as well as rich opportunities. Postmodernism's challenge for Christianity differs from that of modernism. Modernists would argue that Christianity is not true, while postmodernists would critique Christianity for claiming that Christianity is unique. While there is a conservative or restorationist postmodernism, there is also a deconstructive postmodernism that denies the objectivity involved in foundationalism.

Post-Reformation. The ongoing efforts in the seventeenth and eighteenth centuries to bring about doctrinal and ecclesiastical reforms in the churches, resulting in denominational divisions and diverse theological emphases.

Reformation. European Christian movement in the sixteenth century that brought about reforms of doctrine, practices, and structures in the Roman Catholic Church.

Revelation. An uncovering, a removal of the veil, a disclosure of what was previously unknown. Also, God's manifestation of himself to humankind in such a way that men and women can know and have fellowship with him.

Rule of Faith. A principle that was employed in the early church to evaluate and test theological opinions for their consistency with the doctrine that was widely accepted as apostolic tradition, best exemplified in the Apostles' Creed and the Nicene Creed.

Sensus Plenior. A Latin term pointing to the fuller meaning of a passage of Scripture as intended by God, but not clearly or fully understood by the human author or the original hearers/readers.

Sola Scriptura. A Latin phrase meaning "Scripture alone," pointing to the Bible as the primary authority for all things necessary to know, believe, and observe for salvation.

Special Revelation. God's self-manifestation in a particular way to particular people at particular times and places. God's special revelation is most fully made known to humans through the life, work, and teachings of Jesus Christ (John 1:14, 18; Col. 1:15–18; Heb. 1:1–3).

Typological Interpretation. From the Greek *typos*: pattern or archetype. It represents an approach to biblical interpretation in which persons, events, or things of the Old Testament are interpreted as foreshadowings or prototypes of persons, events, or things in the New Testament. Typological interpretation differs from allegorical interpretation in that typology understands a revelatory connection between two historically distinct but religiously significant persons or events, whereas allegory looks for a deeper, hidden, spiritual meaning in the text without an obvious connection to the text being interpreted.

Vulgate. A late fourth-century Latin translation of the Bible, largely the work of Jerome (ca. 341–420).

RESOURCES FOR FURTHER STUDY

Bray, Gerald. *Biblical Interpretation, Past and Present*. Downers Grove, IL: InterVarsity, 2000.

———. *Creeds, Councils, and Christ*. Downers Grove, IL: InterVarsity, 1984.

Brown, Colin. *Christianity and Western Thought*. 2 vols. Downers Grove, IL: InterVarsity, 1984.

Brown, Harold O. J. *Heresies: Heresy and Orthodoxy in the History of the Church*. Garden City, NY: Doubleday, 1984.

Burtchaell, James. *The Dying of the Light: The Disengagement of Colleges and Universities from Their Christian Churches*. Grand Rapids, MI: Eerdmans, 1998.

Craig, William Lane. *Reasonable Faith*. Third edition. Wheaton, IL: Crossway, 2008.

Dockery, David S. *Biblical Interpretation Then and Now*. Grand Rapids, MI: Baker, 1992.

———. *Renewing Minds: Serving Church and Society through Christian Higher Education*. Nashville: Broadman, 2007–2008.

———., editor. *Faith and Learning: A Handbook for Christian Higher Education*. Nashville: Broadman, 2012.

George, Timothy. *Theology of the Reformers*. Nashville: Broadman, 1988.

Gonzales, Justo. *A History of Christian Thought*. Nashville: Abingdon, 1975.

Hauerwas, Stanley. *The State of the University: Academic Knowledge and the Knowledge of God*. Oxford: Blackwell, 2007.

Hill, Jonathan. *What Has Christianity Ever Done for Us?* Downers Grove, IL: InterVarsity, 2005.

Holmes, Arthur. *Building the Christian Academy*. Grand Rapids, MI: Eerdmans, 2001.

Howard, Thomas A., editor. *The Future of Christian Learning*. Grand Rapids, MI: Brazos, 2008.

Keen, Ralph. *The Christian Tradition*. Lanham, MD: Rowman & Littlefield, 2004.

Kronman, Anthony. *Education's End: Why Our Colleges and Universities Have Given Up on the Meaning of Life.* New Haven, CT: Yale University Press, 2008.

Litfin, Duane. *Conceiving the Christian College.* Grand Rapids, MI: Eerdmans, 2004.

Marsden, George M. *The Outrageous Idea of Christian Scholarship.* Oxford, UK: Oxford University Press, 1998.

———. *The Soul of the American University: From Protestant Establishment to Established Nonbelief.* New York: Oxford University Press, 1996.

McGrath, Alister. *Heresy: A History of Defending the Truth.* New York: Harper One, 2009.

Neuhaus, Richard John. "A University of a Particular Kind." *First Things* (April 2007).

Newman, John Henry. *The Idea of a University.* Reprint. London: Longman, Green, 1907.

Oden, Thomas. *How Africa Shaped the Christian Mind.* Downers Grove, IL: InterVarsity, 2010.

———. *The Rebirth of Orthodoxy.* New York: HarperCollins, 2003.

Packer, J. I., and Thomas Oden. *One Faith: The Evangelical Consensus.* Downers Grove, IL: InterVarsity, 2004.

Pelikan, Jaroslav. *Credo: Historical and Theological Guide to Creeds and Confessions of Faith in the Christian Tradition.* New Haven, CT: Yale University Press, 2005.

———. *The Idea of a University: A Reexamination.* New Haven, CT: Yale University Press, 1992.

Piper, John. *Think: The Life of the Mind and the Love of God.* Wheaton, IL: Crossway, 2010.

Poe, Harry L. *Christianity in the Academy.* Grand Rapids, MI: Baker, 2004.

Pope John Paul II. *Ex Corde Ecclesiae: On Catholic Universities.* Encyclical Letter, 1990.

Spliesgant, Roland, et al. *A History of Christianity in Asia, Africa, and Latin America.* Grand Rapids, MI: Eerdmans, 2007.

Taylor, Charles. *A Secular Age.* Cambridge, UK: Belknap, 2007.

Tennant, Timothy. *Theology in the Context of World Christianity*. Grand Rapids, MI: Zondervan, 2007.

Turner, H. E. W. *The Pattern of Christian Truth*. London: Mowbray, 1954.

Wilken, Robert L. "The Christian Intellectual Tradition." *First Things* (June/ July 1991).

Wilkens, Steve, and Alan Padgett. *Christianity and Western Thought*. 2 vols. Downers Grove, IL: InterVarsity, 2000.

CONSULTING EDITORS

Hunter Baker
Timothy George
Niel Nielson
Philip G. Ryken
Michael J. Wilkins
John D. Woodbridge

GENERAL INDEX

✚ RECLAIMING THE CHRISTIAN INTELLECTUAL TRADITION SERIES

For more information, visit **crossway.org**.